THE
ANGEL
OF THE
LORD

Other titles available by Laurence M. Vance:

The Other Side of Calvinism
A Brief History of English Bible Translations

THE
ANGEL
OF THE
LORD

by

Laurence M. Vance, B.D., Th.M., Th.D.

Vance Publications
Pensacola, FL

ISBN 0-9628898-2-2
Library of Congress Catalog Card Number: 94-90190

Published and Distributed by: Vance Publications
P.O. Box 11781, Pensacola, FL 32524, 904-474-1626

Printed in the United States of America

TABLE OF CONTENTS

PREFACE

Who is the angel of the Lord and what is his relationship to other angels and God himself? A relatively simply question it might be inferred. Yet the actual term itself occurs in the Bible fifty-nine times in fifty-eight verses, and is found throughout eleven books of the Old Testament and three of the New. The relative importance, however, of any biblical doctrine is not determined by the magnitude of its occurrence in the pages of the Bible. Conversely, the want of voluminous material does not render any dogma less significant. The virgin birth, for example, although a cardinal point of faith since it is necessitated by the declaration of Christ's deity, is certainly not specifically mentioned in more than a handful of places. Since **"All scripture is given by inspiration of God, and is profitable for doctrine, for reproof, for correction, for instruction in righteousness"** (2 Tim 3:16), it behooves us to examine each and every doctrine, precept, and principle with the same diligence and comprehensiveness.

The authority for all assertions presented and conclusions drawn will be the Holy Bible. Pagan superstitions will not be introduced as plausible and no attempt will be made to chronicle ancient legends. Secular impressions and humanistic sentiments are impertinent to our study. Jewish theological speculations are irrelevant and Christian presuppositions are of no consequence. Accordingly, the emphasis of this treatise will be on what the Bible veritably says. This means that any presentation of these unbiblical sources is for the sake of its correction and our amusement, not its advancement and our instruction. We are really only interested in the exact, literal, precise, definite meaning of what the Bible specifically and unequivocally states. This entails both a meticulous and methodical approach to our understanding of the subject of the angel of the Lord. The perspicuity of the Scripture being maintained, no new hermeneutic will be inaugurated; no innovative exegesis will be presented; no exercises in semantics will be required.

Although there are several reasons for the undertaking of a work such as this, the defense of the deity of the Lord Jesus Christ certainly stands at the forefront. A study of the angel of the Lord provides us with one of the greatest proofs that **"God was manifest in the flesh"** (1 Tim 3:16). This defense is necessary for two reasons. The proliferation of cults and sects with their revived Christological heresies in and of itself definitely merits an apologia. But the appalling ignorance of theology and ignominious apathy toward doctrine of the modern-day Christian provides even greater incentive. Considered theologically, this biblically-based examination of the angel of the Lord finds its background in Angelology and its fulfillment in Christology. From a practical standpoint, however, it seeks to assemble all the available biblical data concerning angels into one convenient source where the Bible is allowed to speak for itself and subsequently correct all errors, fallacies, and misconceptions of men.

The work can basically be divided into two parts: angels and the angel of the Lord. Scripture quotes in the main will be given in full since they are the foundation of all knowledge. They are therefore meant to be read, inasmuch as they form such an intrinsic part of the narrative. Footnotes will be kept to a minimum and are strictly for reference; all exegesis, critique, and analysis will be handled within the text. No attempt is made to be eclectic and all-encompassing, only scriptural; and no apology is offered for inclusiveness and partiality.

CHAPTER ONE

AN ANGELIC SURVEY

By way of introduction, and since the volume of material in the Bible concerning angels is both diverse and substantial, a general angelic survey is in order to lay the groundwork for our study. The word angel, in one form or another, occurs 297 times in 283 verses. 117 of these instances are in 108 verses of the Old Testament, while the New Testament makes mention of angels 180 times in 175 verses. Angels can be found in seventeen books of the Old Testament and eighteen of the New. The classification and characterization of angels is found throughout the Scripture, but often times no further description is given other than the bare mention of an angel or angels. Since the biblical references to angels are varied and recurrently ambiguous, this survey is necessarily informative and inaugurative, rather than interpretive and instructive.

The angel of the Lord

As stated previously, the angel of the Lord is mentioned in the Bible fifty-nine times in fifty-eight verses, and is found throughout eleven books of the Old Testament and three of the New. This denotation of an angel is the most frequent one appearing in the Bible. The are twenty-one distinct presentations of the angel of the Lord, the most common being a direct appearance:

> **And the angel of the LORD appeared unto him in a flame of fire out of the midst of a bush: and he looked, and, behold, the bush burned with fire, and the bush was not consumed. -- Exo 3:2**

> **And the angel of the LORD appeared unto him, and said unto him, The LORD is with thee, thou mighty man of valour. -- Judg 6:12**

Additional manifestations of the angel of the Lord include something he does or says:

> **And it came to pass that night, that the angel of the LORD went out, and smote in the camp of the Assyrians an hundred fourscore and five thousand: and when they arose early in the morning, behold, they were all dead corpses. -- 2 Ki 19:35**

> **And the angel of the LORD called unto him out of heaven, and said, Abraham, Abraham: and he said, Here am I. -- Gen 22:11**

At times the angel of the Lord is also designated or referenced with some other angelic term and occasionally he is described without the use of the word *angel* at all. These will not be considered generally here, but in particular later.

An angel of the Lord

The Bible also furnishes us with nine occurrences in eight verses of *an angel of the Lord.* Although this angel spake to the children of Israel (Judg 2:1-4), he customarily appeared to individuals:

> **And when Gideon perceived that he was an angel of the LORD, Gideon said, Alas, O Lord GOD! for because I have seen an angel of the LORD face to face. -- Judg 6:22**

> **But the angel of the LORD did no more appear to Manoah and to his wife. Then Manoah knew that he was an angel of the LORD. -- Judg 13:21**

> **But when Herod was dead, behold, an angel of the Lord appeareth in a dream to Joseph in Egypt, -- Mat 2:19**

Whether or not this angel of the Lord is one individual, as well as his relationship to the angel of the Lord, remains to be seen.

Angels in General

Like the existence of God, the reality of angels is presupposed by the Bible. Although the angel of the Lord is mentioned initially in Genesis 16, the first reference to angels in general occurs in Genesis 19:

> **And there came two angels to Sodom at even; and Lot sat in the gate of Sodom: and Lot seeing them rose up to meet them; and he bowed himself with his face toward the ground; -- Gen 19:1**

Here we see the fact that these were angels was known and accepted without any explanation of who they were, where they were from, or what their intended purpose was. This is commonplace throughout the Bible, where forty times the bare actuality of angels is recorded. This broad use of angels can be put into two categories. Besides the two angels who visited Lot, there are several other places where a definite number of angels is mentioned in a general, nondescript fashion:

> **And seeth two angels in white sitting, the one at the head, and the other at the feet, where the body of Jesus had lain. -- John 20:12**

> **And after these things I saw four angels standing on the four corners of the earth, holding the four winds of the earth, that the wind should not blow on the earth, nor on the sea, nor on any tree. -- Rev 7:1**

> **And had a wall great and high, and had twelve gates, and at the gates twelve angels, and names written thereon, which are the names of the twelve tribes of the children of Israel: -- Rev 21:12**

The prevailing manner, however, in which angels are presented throughout the Bible is indefinite and indistinct:

> **And he was there in the wilderness forty days, tempted of Satan; and was with the wild beasts; and the angels ministered unto him. -- Mark 1:13**

> And it came to pass, that the beggar died, and
> was carried by the angels into Abraham's
> bosom: the rich man also died, and was buried;
> -- Luke 16:22

> Be not forgetful to entertain strangers: for
> thereby some have entertained angels un-
> awares. -- Heb 13:2

Although still spoken of in a general fashion, there
are numerous passages where a single angel in particular is mentioned indiscriminately. This takes one of two
forms. Ten times we read of simply an angel with no
further descriptive information given. Only two of these
are in the Old Testament:

> Behold, I send an Angel before thee, to keep
> thee in the way, and to bring thee into the
> place which I have prepared. -- Exo 23:20

> He said unto him, I am a prophet also as thou
> art; and an angel spake unto me by the word of
> the LORD, saying, Bring him back with thee
> into thine house, that he may eat bread and
> drink water. But he lied unto him. -- 1 Ki 13:18

The rest, which are distributed among the Gospels, Acts,
and Revelation, thrice concern a vain reference such as
found in the Old Testament:

> The people therefore, that stood by, and heard
> it, said that it thundered: others said, An angel
> spake to him. -- John 12:29

> And all that sat in the council, looking sted-
> fastly on him, saw his face as it had been the
> face of an angel. -- Acts 6:15

> And there arose a great cry: and the scribes
> that were of the Pharisees' part arose, and
> strove, saying, We find no evil in this man: but
> if a spirit or an angel hath spoken to him, let us
> not fight against God. -- Acts 23:9

Twice, however, actual events that do in fact take place
are described:

> And there appeared an angel unto him from
> heaven, strengthening him. -- Luke 22:43

> **For an angel went down at a certain season into the pool, and troubled the water: whosoever then first after the troubling of the water stepped in was made whole of whatsoever disease he had. -- John 5:4**

And three times it is a future, albeit certain, event that is to occur:

> **And I beheld, and heard an angel flying through the midst of heaven, saying with a loud voice, Woe, woe, woe, to the inhabiters of the earth by reason of the other voices of the trumpet of the three angels, which are yet to sound! -- Rev 8:13**

> **And I saw an angel standing in the sun; and he cried with a loud voice, saying to all the fowls that fly in the midst of heaven, Come and gather yourselves together unto the supper of the great God; -- Rev 19:17**

> **And I saw an angel come down from heaven, having the key of the bottomless pit and a great chain in his hand. -- Rev 20:1**

The second type of appearance of a lone angel is that in which *another angel* is referred to. Naturally, this usually involves the connection of another angel to one or more angels previously alluded to:

> **And, behold, the angel that talked with me went forth, and another angel went out to meet him, -- Zec 2:3**

> **And I saw another angel ascending from the east, having the seal of the living God: and he cried with a loud voice to the four angels, to whom it was given to hurt the earth and the sea, -- Rev 7:2**

There are eight other occurrences, all in Revelation, of *another angel,* plus one case where the addition of two other angels labels the last the *third angel* (Rev 14:9).

Specific angels

In contrast to the often ambiguous general mention

of angels throughout the Bible, there are twenty-one occasions in which a specific angel (or angels) is introduced, although perhaps not described, and sometimes never to be referred to again. In the Old Testament we find two examples that are candidates for the angel of the Lord:

> **The Angel which redeemed me from all evil, bless the lads; and let my name be named on them, and the name of my fathers Abraham and Isaac; and let them grow into a multitude in the midst of the earth. -- Gen 48:16**

> **In all their affliction he was afflicted, and the angel of his presence saved them: in his love and in his pity he redeemed them; and he bare them, and carried them all the days of old. -- Isa 63:9**

There are also three situations where an angel termed *his angel* is distinctively associated with God:

> **The LORD God of heaven, which took me from my father's house, and from the land of my kindred, and which spake unto me, and that sware unto me, saying, Unto thy seed will I give this land; he shall send his angel before thee, and thou shalt take a wife unto my son from thence. -- Gen 24:7**

> **Then Nebuchadnezzar spake, and said, Blessed be the God of Shadrach, Meshach, and Abednego, who hath sent his angel, and delivered his servants that trusted in him, and have changed the king's word, and yielded their bodies, that they might not serve nor worship any god, except their own God. -- Dan 3:28**

> **My God hath sent his angel, and hath shut the lions' mouths, that they have not hurt me: forasmuch as before him innocency was found in me; and also before thee, O king, have I done no hurt. -- Dan 6:22**

Twice, however, the possible identification is cryptic and puzzling:

> **Suffer not thy mouth to cause thy flesh to sin;**

neither say thou before the angel, that it was an error: wherefore should God be angry at thy voice, and destroy the work of thine hands? -- Eccl 5:6

Then said I, O my lord, what are these? And the angel that talked with me said unto me, I will show thee what these be. -- Zec 1:9

Confining ourselves to the New Testament, we are introduced eight times to heretofore unknown angels. Two are mentioned either by name or association:

And in the sixth month the angel Gabriel was sent from God unto a city of Galilee, named Nazareth, -- Luke 1:26

The Revelation of Jesus Christ, which God gave unto him, to show unto his servants things which must shortly come to pass; and he sent and signified it by his angel unto his servant John: -- Rev 1:1

But it is in the book of Revelation that we are really presented with a diverse company of angels:

The mystery of the seven stars which thou sawest in my right hand, and the seven golden candlesticks. The seven stars are the angels of the seven churches: and the seven candlesticks which thou sawest are the seven churches. -- Rev 1:20

And I saw the seven angels which stood before God; and to them were given seven trumpets. -- Rev 8:2

And they had a king over them, which is the angel of the bottomless pit, whose name in the Hebrew tongue is Abaddon, but in the Greek tongue hath his name Apollyon. -- Rev 9:11

Saying to the sixth angel which had the trumpet, Loose the four angels which are bound in the great river Euphrates. -- Rev 9:14

And I saw another sign in heaven, great and marvellous, seven angels having the seven last plagues; for in them is filled up the wrath of God. -- Rev 15:1

> And I heard the angel of the waters say, Thou
> art righteous, O Lord, which art, and wast, and
> shalt be, because thou hast judged thus. -- Rev
> 16:5

There is one case of a specific angel who transcends
both Testaments, but whether or not this angel is one
and the same everywhere he his mentioned remains to
be determined:

> And God heard the voice of the lad; and the
> angel of God called to Hagar out of heaven, and
> said unto her, What aileth thee, Hagar? fear
> not; for God hath heard the voice of the lad
> where he is. -- Gen 21:17

> And the angel of God spake unto me in a
> dream, saying, Jacob: And I said, Here am I. --
> Gen 31:11

> And the angel of God, which went before the
> camp of Israel, removed and went behind
> them; and the pillar of the cloud went from
> before their face, and stood behind them: -- Exo
> 14:19

> And the angel of God said unto him, Take the
> flesh and the unleavened cakes, and lay them
> upon this rock, and pour out the broth. And he
> did so. -- Judg 6:20

> And God hearkened to the voice of Manoah;
> and the angel of God came again unto the
> woman as she sat in the field: but Manoah her
> husband was not with her. -- Judg 13:9

> For there stood by me this night the angel of
> God, whose I am, and whom I serve, -- Acts
> 27:23

The relationship of this angel to the angel of the Lord is
also apropos and demands further inquiry.

Descriptive angels

Although their general mention is the chief occurrence of angels in the Bible, there are several passages
that describe a certain class of angels by particular

characteristics without hinting as to their number or organization. The most numerous case of descriptive angels are those depicted as holy:

> **And they said, Cornelius the centurion, a just man, and one that feareth God, and of good report among all the nation of the Jews, was warned from God by an holy angel to send for thee into his house, and to hear words of thee. -- Acts 10:22**

> **The same shall drink of the wine of the wrath of God, which is poured out without mixture into the cup of his indignation; and he shall be tormented with fire and brimstone in the presence of the holy angels, and in the presence of the Lamb: -- Rev 14:10**

> **Whosoever therefore shall be ashamed of me and of my words in this adulterous and sinful generation; of him also shall the Son of man be ashamed, when he cometh in the glory of his Father with the holy angels. -- Mark 8:38**

This representation of angels is found five times with three of these references appearing in parallel passages in the Gospels.

Another graphic term concerning angels speaks of their potent nobility:

> **And I saw another mighty angel come down from heaven, clothed with a cloud: and a rainbow was upon his head, and his face was as it were the sun, and his feet as pillars of fire: -- Rev 10:1**

> **And a mighty angel took up a stone like a great millstone, and cast it into the sea, saying, Thus with violence shall that great city Babylon be thrown down, and shall be found no more at all. -- Rev 18:21**

> **And to you who are troubled rest with us, when the Lord Jesus shall be revealed from heaven with his mighty angels, -- 2 Th 1:7**

The portrayal of angels as mighty occurs but three times in the Scripture.

There are three occasions in which there is but one instance of an angel being termed in a specific fashion:

> I charge thee before God, and the Lord Jesus Christ, and the elect angels, that thou observe these things without preferring one before another, doing nothing by partiality. -- 1 Tim 5:21

> He cast upon them the fierceness of his anger, wrath, and indignation, and trouble, by sending evil angels among them. -- Psa 78:49

> And I saw a strong angel proclaiming with a loud voice, Who is worthy to open the book, and to loose the seals thereof? -- Rev 5:2

The hitherto mention of descriptive angels does not exemplify any angel as an individual. There is one appellation, however, that applies to a particular angel and him alone:

> For the Lord himself shall descend from heaven with a shout, with the voice of the archangel, and with the trump of God: and the dead in Christ shall rise first: -- 1 Th 4:16

> Yet Michael the archangel, when contending with the devil he disputed about the body of Moses, durst not bring against him a railing accusation, but said, The Lord rebuke thee. -- Jude 1:9

Although there are three other instances where Michael is referred to, these are the only two occasions in the Bible where this archangel is so named.

Designative angels

Reciprocal to the descriptive characteristics of angels, excepting the adjectival form, are those biblical verses that associate various angels with someone or some location or action. Once again their quantity and order remains a mystery. Of those relating angels to someone, the use of the pronoun *his* or *their* is employed. The most numerous of these is that of angels connected with God:

Behold, he put no trust in his servants; and his angels he charged with folly: -- Job 4:18

For he shall give his angels charge over thee, to keep thee in all thy ways. -- Psa 91:11

Bless the LORD, ye his angels, that excel in strength, that do his commandments, hearkening unto the voice of his word. -- Psa 103:20

Who maketh his angels spirits; his ministers a flaming fire: -- Psa 104:4

Praise ye him, all his angels: praise ye him, all his hosts. -- Psa 148:2

And saith unto him, If thou be the Son of God, cast thyself down: for it is written, He shall give his angels charge concerning thee: and in their hands they shall bear thee up, lest at any time thou dash thy foot against a stone. -- Mat 4:6

For it is written, He shall give his angels charge over thee, to keep thee: -- Luke 4:10

And of the angels he saith, Who maketh his angels spirits, and his ministers a flame of fire. -- Heb 1:7

He that overcometh, the same shall be clothed in white raiment; and I will not blot out his name out of the book of life, but I will confess his name before my Father, and before his angels. -- Rev 3:5

A similar situation concerns those angels said to be identified with the Lord Jesus Christ:

The Son of man shall send forth his angels, and they shall gather out of his kingdom all things that offend, and them which do iniquity; -- Mat 13:41

For the Son of man shall come in the glory of his Father with his angels; and then he shall reward every man according to his works. -- Mat 16:27

And he shall send his angels with a great sound of a trumpet, and they shall gather together his elect from the four winds, from

> one end of heaven to the other. -- Mat 24:31

> And then shall he send his angels, and shall gather together his elect from the four winds, from the uttermost part of the earth to the uttermost part of heaven. -- Mark 13:27

> And to you who are troubled rest with us, when the Lord Jesus shall be revealed from heaven with his mighty angels, -- 2 Th 1:7

The devil likewise has his angels:

> Then shall he say also unto them on the left hand, Depart from me, ye cursed, into everlasting fire, prepared for the devil and his angels: -- Mat 25:41

> And there was war in heaven: Michael and his angels fought against the dragon; and the dragon fought and his angels, -- Rev 12:7

> And the great dragon was cast out, that old serpent, called the Devil, and Satan, which deceiveth the whole world: he was cast out into the earth, and his angels were cast out with him. -- Rev 12:9

The other two cases of *his angels* refer respectively to Michael and the supposed apparition of a dead man:

> And there was war in heaven: Michael and his angels fought against the dragon; and the dragon fought and his angels, -- Rev 12:7

> And they said unto her, Thou art mad. But she constantly affirmed that it was even so. Then said they, It is his angel. -- Acts 12:15

The sole instance of the pronoun *their* as designating an angel involves the idea of a guardian angel:

> Take heed that ye despise not one of these little ones; for I say unto you, That in heaven their angels do always behold the face of my Father which is in heaven. -- Mat 18:10

Since God has his angels, it is therefore natural that they should be termed the *angels of God*. This designation is found in the Bible eight times:

And he dreamed, and behold a ladder set up on the earth, and the top of it reached to heaven: and behold the angels of God ascending and descending on it. -- Gen 28:12

And Jacob went on his way, and the angels of God met him. -- Gen 32:1

For in the resurrection they neither marry, nor are given in marriage, but are as the angels of God in heaven. -- Mat 22:30

Also I say unto you, Whosoever shall confess me before men, him shall the Son of man also confess before the angels of God: -- Luke 12:8

But he that denieth me before men shall be denied before the angels of God. -- Luke 12:9

Likewise, I say unto you, there is joy in the presence of the angels of God over one sinner that repenteth. -- Luke 15:10

And he saith unto him, Verily, verily, I say unto you, Hereafter ye shall see heaven open, and the angels of God ascending and descending upon the Son of man. -- John 1:51

And again, when he bringeth in the firstbegotten into the world, he saith, And let all the angels of God worship him. -- Heb 1:6

When an individual angel of God makes an appearance, he is instinctively called *an angel of God.* This occurs five times in the Old Testament where each instance is presented in the context of a simile:

Then the woman came and told her husband, saying, A man of God came unto me, and his countenance was like the countenance of an angel of God, very terrible: but I asked him not whence he was, neither told he me his name: -- Judg 13:6

And Achish answered and said to David, I know that thou art good in my sight, as an angel of God: notwithstanding the princes of the Philistines have said, He shall not go up with us to the battle. -- 1 Sam 29:9

Then thine handmaid said, The word of my

lord the king shall now be comfortable: for as an angel of God, so is my lord the king to discern good and bad: therefore the LORD thy God will be with thee. -- 2 Sam 14:17

To fetch about this form of speech hath thy servant Joab done this thing: and my lord is wise, according to the wisdom of an angel of God, to know all things that are in the earth. -- 2 Sam 14:20

And he hath slandered thy servant unto my lord the king; but my lord the king is as an angel of God: do therefore what is good in thine eyes. -- 2 Sam 19:27

There are also two examples of an angel of God in the New Testament:

He saw in a vision evidently about the ninth hour of the day an angel of God coming in to him, and saying unto him, Cornelius. -- Acts 10:3

And my temptation which was in my flesh ye despised not, nor rejected; but received me as an angel of God, even as Christ Jesus. -- Gal 4:14

There are found exclusively in the New Testament five references relating angels to a location. This location is always heaven; the relationship is just expressed in different ways:

For in the resurrection they neither marry, nor are given in marriage, but are as the angels of God in heaven. -- Mat 22:30

But of that day and hour knoweth no man, no, not the angels of heaven, but my Father only. -- Mat 24:36

For when they shall rise from the dead, they neither marry, nor are given in marriage; but are as the angels which are in heaven. -- Mark 12:25

But of that day and that hour knoweth no man, no, not the angels which are in heaven, neither the Son, but the Father. -- Mark 13:32

But though we, or an angel from heaven, preach any other gospel unto you than that which we have preached unto you, let him be accursed. -- Gal 1:8

The last three cases of designative angels are all related to some evil connotation:

For if God spared not the angels that sinned, but cast them down to hell, and delivered them into chains of darkness, to be reserved unto judgment; -- 2 Pet 2:4

And the angels which kept not their first estate, but left their own habitation, he hath reserved in everlasting chains under darkness unto the judgment of the great day. -- Jude 1:6

And no marvel; for Satan himself is transformed into an angel of light. -- 2 Cor 11:14

There are a total of forty-three occasions where an angel is designated by association with someone or some location or action.

Referring angels

In addition to the aforementioned descriptions and designations of angels in general and specific angels in particular, there are certain references in the Bible to angels that merely allude to an angel previously mentioned or refer to an angel introduced in the context. These are typically articular in nature and include the bare article, the article with a description, as well as the article with a numerical denomination. Twenty-nine times we find *the angel* or *the angels* mentioned alone with no further graphic data. The bulk of these in the Old Testament refer to the angel of the Lord:

So Manoah took a kid with a meat offering, and offered it upon a rock unto the LORD: and the angel did wonderously; and Manoah and his wife looked on. -- Judg 13:19

And when the angel stretched out his hand upon Jerusalem to destroy it, the LORD re-

pented him of the evil, and said to the angel that destroyed the people, It is enough: stay now thine hand. And the angel of the LORD was by the threshingplace of Araunah the Jebusite. -- 2 Sam 24:16

And Ornan turned back, and saw the angel; and his four sons with him hid themselves. Now Ornan was threshing wheat. -- 1 Chr 21:20

And the LORD commanded the angel; and he put up his sword again into the sheath thereof. -- 1 Chr 21:27

Yea, he had power over the angel, and prevailed: he wept, and made supplication unto him: he found him in Bethel, and there he spake with us; -- Hosea 12:4

Now Joshua was clothed with filthy garments, and stood before the angel. -- Zec 3:3

The lone reference to *the angels* in the Old Testament (Gen 19:15) can be ascribed to the first occurrence of angels in the Bible: **"And there came two angels to Sodom"** (Gen 19:1). The last instance of this type (Zec 6:5) refers to the specific angel that Zechariah affirmed **"talked with me"** (Zec 6:4).

On three occasions in the New Testament the angel of the Lord is mentioned and subsequently cited by the term *the angel:*

And the angel answered and said unto the women, Fear not ye: for I know that ye seek Jesus, which was crucified. -- Mat 28:5

And the angel said unto them, Fear not: for, behold, I bring you good tidings of great joy, which shall be to all people. -- Luke 2:10

And the angel said unto him, Gird thyself, and bind on thy sandals. And so he did. And he saith unto him, Cast thy garment about thee, and follow me. And he went out, and followed him; and wist not that it was true which was done by the angel; but thought he saw a vision. When they were past the first and the second ward, they came unto the iron gate that

leadeth unto the city; which opened to them of his own accord: and they went out, and passed on through one street; and forthwith the angel departed from him. -- Acts 12:8-10

There are eight articular references in Luke chapter one that relate directly to **"the angel Gabriel"** (Luke 1:26) and one in Luke 2:15 that refers to **"a multitude of the heavenly host"** (Luke 2:13). The rest are in Revelation and advert once each (Rev 8:5, 14:19) respectively to the angel **"having a golden censer"** (Rev 8:3) and the one with **"a sharp sickle"** (Rev 14:17), twice (Rev 17:7, 21:17) to **"one of the seven angels which had the seven vials"** (Rev 17:1), and three times (Rev 10:9,10, 11:1) to the angel that John saw stand **"upon the sea and upon the earth"** (Rev 10:5).

Frequently *the angel* is given with a further explanation so as to better determine what it is in reference to. The angel of the Lord is alluded to five times.

And when the angel stretched out his hand upon Jerusalem to destroy it, the LORD repented him of the evil, and said to the angel that destroyed the people, It is enough: stay now thine hand. And the angel of the LORD was by the threshingplace of Araunah the Jebusite. And David spake unto the LORD when he saw the angel that smote the people, and said, Lo, I have sinned, and I have done wickedly: but these sheep, what have they done? let thine hand, I pray thee, be against me, and against my father's house. -- 2 Sam 24:16-17

And God sent an angel unto Jerusalem to destroy it: and as he was destroying, the LORD beheld, and he repented him of the evil, and said to the angel that destroyed, It is enough, stay now thine hand. And the angel of the LORD stood by the threshingfloor of Ornan the Jebusite. -- 1 Chr 21:15

In all their affliction he was afflicted, and the angel of his presence saved them: in his love and in his pity he redeemed them; and he bare

**them, and carried them all the days of old. --
Isa 63:9**

**This Moses whom they refused, saying, Who
made thee a ruler and a judge? the same did
God send to be a ruler and a deliverer by the
hand of the angel which appeared to him in the
bush. -- Acts 7:35**

**This is he, that was in the church in the
wilderness with the angel which spake to him
in the mount Sina, and with our fathers: who
received the lively oracles to give unto us: --
Acts 7:38**

Twice we read of angelic events that occurred in the
past:

**For if God spared not the angels that sinned,
but cast them down to hell, and delivered them
into chains of darkness, to be reserved unto
judgment; -- 2 Pet 2:4**

**And the angels which kept not their first
estate, but left their own habitation, he hath
reserved in everlasting chains under darkness
unto the judgment of the great day. -- Jude 1:6**

Other instances of this explanatory referral include **"the
angel which spake unto Cornelius"** (Acts 10:7), the
angel that Zechariah said **"talked with me"** (Zec
1:13,19, 2:3, 4:1,4,5, 5:5,10, 6:4) or **"communed with
me"** (Zec 1:14), the angel that John saw stand **"upon
the sea and upon the earth"** (Rev 10:5,8), another
angel that John maintained **"shewed me these things"**
(Rev 22:8), and the **"angels of the seven churches"**
(Rev 1:20) found in Revelation chapter two and three.

It is the book of Revelation, since it abounds with the
mention of angels, that furnishes us with the only cases
of the numerical elucidation of angels. The main angels
detailed are as follows:

**And after these things I saw four angels
standing on the four corners of the earth,
holding the four winds of the earth, that the
wind should not blow on the earth, nor on the
sea, nor on any tree. -- Rev 7:1**

> **And I saw the seven angels which stood before God; and to them were given seven trumpets. -- Rev 8:2**

> **Saying to the sixth angel which had the trumpet, Loose the four angels which are bound in the great river Euphrates. -- Rev 9:14**

> **And I saw another sign in heaven, great and marvellous, seven angels having the seven last plagues; for in them is filled up the wrath of God. -- Rev 15:1**

The **"four angels standing on the four courners of the earth"** (Rev 7:1) are cited one time (Rev 7:2), as are (Rev 9:15) **"the four angels which are bound in the great river Euphrates"** (Rev 9:14). The **"seven angels which stood before God"** (Rev 8:2) are referred to once as a group (Rev 8:6), once as a portion of the whole: **"the three angels, which are yet to sound"** (Rev 8:13), and once each as individuals: **"the first angel"** (Rev 8:7), **"the second angel"** (Rev 8:8), **"the third angel"** (Rev 8:10), **"the fourth angel"** (Rev 8:12), **"the fifth angel"** (Rev 9:1), excepting the sixth (Rev 9:13,14) and seventh (Rev 10:7, 11:15), which are alluded to twice. The **"seven angels having the seven last plagues"** (Rev 15:1) are addressed four times as a group (Rev 15:6,7,8, 16:1), and likewise, excepting the first, as individuals: **"the second angel"** (Rev 16:3), **"the third angel"** (Rev 16:4), **"the fourth angel"** (Rev 10:8), **"the fifth angel"** (Rev 16:10), **"the sixth angel"** (Rev 16:12), **"the seventh angel"** (Rev 16:17). There are also two occasions in which an unidentified **"one of the seven"** is mentioned (Rev 17:1, 21:9).

The anarthrous use of angel to refer back to an angel previously mentioned or introduced is analogous to the articular usance. This time all of the references in the Old Testament are to the angel of the Lord:

> **And I will send an angel before thee; and I will drive out the Canaanite, the Amorite, and the Hittite, and the Perizzite, the Hivite, and the Jebusite: -- Exo 33:2**

> And when we cried unto the LORD, he heard our voice, and sent an angel, and hath brought us forth out of Egypt: and, behold, we are in Kadesh, a city in the uttermost of thy border: -- Num 20:16

> And as he lay and slept under a juniper tree, behold, then an angel touched him, and said unto him, Arise and eat. -- 1 Ki 19:5

> And God sent an angel unto Jerusalem to destroy it: and as he was destroying, the LORD beheld, and he repented him of the evil, and said to the angel that destroyed, It is enough, stay now thine hand. And the angel of the LORD stood by the threshingfloor of Ornan the Jebusite. -- 1 Chr 21:15

> And the LORD sent an angel, which cut off all the mighty men of valour, and the leaders and captains in the camp of the king of Assyria. So he returned with shame of face to his own land. And when he was come into the house of his god, they that came forth of his own bowels slew him there with the sword. -- 2 Chr 32:21

Of the two occurrences in New Testament, one averts back to the familiar burning bush in Exodus where the angel of the Lord appeared, although here he is termed **"an angel of the Lord"** (Acts 7:30). The other concerns Peter recounting his trip to Cornelius: **"And he showed us how he had seen an angel in his house, which stood and said unto him, Send men to Joppa, and call for Simon, whose surname is Peter"** (Acts 11:13), and refers to **"an angel of God"** (Acts 10:3).

The third and final way in which an angel is referenced is through the use of a personal pronoun. The first case concerns an angel denominated as *his angel:*

> And he said unto me, The LORD, before whom I walk, will send his angel with thee, and prosper thy way; and thou shalt take a wife for my son of my kindred, and of my father's house: -- Gen 24:40

> And when Peter was come to himself, he said, Now I know of a surety, that the Lord hath

> sent his angel, and hath delivered me out of
> the hand of Herod, and from all the expectation
> of the people of the Jews. -- Acts 12:11

> And he said unto me, These sayings are faithful
> and true: and the Lord God of the holy
> prophets sent his angel to show unto his
> servants the things which must shortly be
> done. -- Rev 22:6

The first of these is Eliezer quoting Abraham, who
previously had made mention of God's angel (Gen 24:7).
The first New Testament reference is to the angel of the
Lord (Acts 12:7) while the second looks back to an initial
mention at the beginning of the book of Revelation.

The other description employed is *mine angel:*

> For mine Angel shall go before thee, and bring
> thee in unto the Amorites, and the Hittites, and
> the Perizzites, and the Canaanites, the Hivites,
> and the Jebusites: and I will cut them off. --
> Exo 23:23

> Therefore now go, lead the people unto the
> place of which I have spoken unto thee: behold,
> mine Angel shall go before thee: nevertheless
> in the day when I visit I will visit their sin
> upon them. -- Exo 32:34

> I Jesus have sent mine angel to testify unto you
> these things in the churches. I am the root and
> the offspring of David, and the bright and
> morning star. -- Rev 22:16

Both of the references in the Old Testament to the angel
that was to go before the children of Israel concern an
unidentified angel mentioned earlier: **"Behold, I send
an Angel before thee, to keep thee in the way, and
to bring thee into the place which I have
prepared"** (Exo 23:20). The angel sent by the Lord
Jesus Christ is the one he introduced at the beginning of
the book of Revelation: **"The Revelation of Jesus
Christ, which God gave unto him, to show unto his
servants things which must shortly come to pass;
and he sent and signified it by his angel unto his
servant John"** (Rev 1:1).

Emphasized angels

Three instances in Old Testament present to us an angel emphasized in the form of an initial capital letter:

> **The Angel which redeemed me from all evil, bless the lads; and let my name be named on them, and the name of my fathers Abraham and Isaac; and let them grow into a multitude in the midst of the earth. -- Gen 48:16**

> **Behold, I send an Angel before thee, to keep thee in the way, and to bring thee into the place which I have prepared. -- Exo 23:20**

> **For mine Angel shall go before thee, and bring thee in unto the Amorites, and the Hittites, and the Perizzites, and the Canaanites, the Hivites, and the Jebusites: and I will cut them off. -- Exo 23:23**

Obviously, this is no ordinary angel. As mentioned previously, the angel in Exodus 23:23 refers back to Exodus 23:20. This leaves two cases of an unidentified angel (or angels), who, due to the nature of his emphasis, demands an explication. This concludes our angelic survey. The characterizations of angels being so diverse, a fuller treatment that is both interpretive and instructive will be necessary before presenting the angel of the Lord.

CHAPTER TWO

THE ANGELS OF GOD

As we saw in the previous chapter, the word *angel*, in one form or another, occurs 297 times in 283 verses. The etymology of the word is quite simple. It comes to us, like so many of our words, through French and Latin, but originally from the Greek *angelos,* signifying a messenger, yet much more since many angels bring no message at all. They can all be scripturally defined as **"ministering spirits"** (Heb 1:14). Consequently, they must make an appearance for anyone to see them. Although our intended purpose is to ascertain the nature and identity of the angel of the Lord, there are still 238 references in 232 verses to angels beside the angel of the Lord. While some of these simply mention him by another name, and others merely refer to a previous account of him, the vast majority inculcate further study of angels since the angel of the Lord is all that an angel is and more. There also exists just as many fallacies and misconceptions about angels in general as there are concerning the angel of the Lord. Therefore, a more detailed examination of the angels of God is in order. This can best be explicated by classifying the available evidence under the headings of their existence, origin, nature, work, and destiny.

The existence of angels

The verity of angels has never been in doubt except in the minds of Atheists and other skeptics, and is maintained by such diverse religions as Islam, Zoroastrianism, Judaism, and Christianity, not to mention the similar ideals of the Hindu and Buddhist, and for that matter most pagan societies. Such an eclectic audience naturally leads to a myriad of contradicting views of not only what an angel does, but what an angel is. Some ideas of the nature and work of angels are as follows:

Generic name for all members of the heavenly host.[1]

Name assigned to the lowest rank in the descending scale of spiritual creatures.[2]

Angels bring prayers of men before God.[3]

Angels punish men.[4]

Angels celebrate with the Church on earth the feasts of Christendom.[5]

The procreation of living creatures could not be explained except by the part of angels.[6]

Every human being has a good and bad angel.[7]

Any of numerous benevolent spiritual beings, powers, or principles that mediate between the realm of the sacred (i.e., the transcendent realm) and the profane realm of time, space, and cause and effect.[8]

To these antiquated superstitions and partial truths could be added equally spurious modern concepts of angels. Their appearance ranges from that of a long-haired, effeminate, winged creature with a halo to that of an extraterrestrial from Star Wars and Star Trek or an alien from some other fanciful science-fiction. Angels typically adorn Christmas cards and assume the form of Cupid, besides frequently appearing in literary works and artistic renderings. The word *angel* is used as a female name and on occasion a male one as well. To be the epitome of innocence and decency is to be—in a figure of speech—an angel. The term is found throughout society, from Los Angeles to Angel Falls in Venezuela (the highest in the world, named after James Angel), from angel food cake to angel dust (phencyclidine or PCP), from angelica wine and trees to angelfish in the seas. Like the Romanist concept of saints, angels are supposed to symbolize and control all facets of life including the days of the week, months of the year, weather, four seasons, hours of the day and night, and phases of the moon. There are also said to be angels of confusion, compassion, and corruption.[9] Some men think that they become angels when they die: glorified human beings. What a convenient way to escape the judgment. The angel Gabriel has been envisioned as teaching Joseph seventy languages overnight.[10] The pseudepigraphical Book of Jubilees claims to have been dictated by an angel to Moses.[11] Perhaps this is where the idea of the angel Moroni and the Book of Mormon came from. Angels have been venerated throughout history and even Mary has been thought to have been an angel![12] And then there is the mock question, never found in Medieval theology,[13] of how many angels could stand on the head of a pin. According to the Bible, none of them could.

It goes without saying that it is not the Bible that has been accepted as the authority for the mass of humanity's knowledge of angels. The sentiments of Philo, Jerome, and Ambrose have been taken, together with Milton's *Paradise Lost,* Dantes' *Divine Comedy,* and the *Celestial Hierarchy* attributed to the sixth-century Dionysius, as the authorities, while the authority of the Bible has been held in contempt. The angels of these fanciful imaginations, together with those of the Koran, Talmud, and Targums, and other traditions, must now give way to the authority of the Bible. Like everywhere else, the existence of angels in the Bible is presupposed, so no time will be wasted in trying to prove their authenticity.

Out of our remaining 238 references to angels, seventy-five can be dismissed as having no relevance due to their being referring in nature only. This in itself does not render them irrelevant, but the fact that their referring is of a bare mention only. This would include two verses in Acts that allude to the angel that came to Cornelius (Acts 10:3-6), four in Luke that reference the angel Gabriel (Luke 1:19), four verses in Zechariah that refer back to **"the angel that talked with me"** (Zec 1:9), and eight locations in Revelation that point to various angels previously mentioned. There also appears, in forty-nine verses, fifty-two mentions of an angel that either refer to the angel of the Lord or make mention of him under another angelic expression. There are four angels mentioned in three verses in the New Testament that are merely quotations, without any additional details, from the Old Testament, plus seven parallel passages in the Gospels that provide no new data. This leaves us with 157 accounts of angels in 153 verses that will be the primary material for our instruction. The number of settings in which these accounts are found is approximately ninety. This is supplemented by supporting verses that appear in the context and various other verses relating to angels. All of these references contain some detail about the origin, nature, work, and destiny of angels. However, some contain much more than others.

The origin of angels

The origin of angels is not difficult to discover, but the accompanying questions of their past and present condition have been cause for much fantasy and fiction. The Bible, however, does provide us with the necessary information to ascertain all the inquiries of their origin through study of their creation, including its verity, time, and purpose, their number, their organization, their abode, and their state, both initially and directly.

Like everything else in existence, contrary to modern science and scientists, angels are the product of God's creation. The testimony of the Bible is clear: if it exists, God created it:

> **Thou, even thou, art LORD alone; thou hast made heaven, the heaven of heavens, with all their host, the earth, and all things that are therein, the seas, and all that is therein, and thou preservest them all; and the host of heaven worshippeth thee. -- Neh 9:6**

> **And when they heard that, they lifted up their
> voice to God with one accord, and said, Lord,
> thou art God, which hast made heaven, and
> earth, and the sea, and all that in them is: --
> Acts 4:24**

The time of their creation, since they are not mentioned
in the narrative of Genesis 1, yet were said to be present
(Job 38:7) when God **"laid the foundations of the
earth"** (Job 38:4), is **"in the beginning"** (Gen 1:1). The
purpose for their creation is manifold, considering all the
various works they have accomplished and do presently
perform. They can all be viewed as either serving God,
worshipping God, or bringing God pleasure:

> **Bless the LORD, ye his angels, that excel in
> strength, that do his commandments, hearken-
> ing unto the voice of his word. -- Psa 103:20**

> **Praise ye him, all his angels: praise ye him, all
> his hosts. -- Psa 148:2**

> **Thou art worthy, O Lord, to receive glory and
> honour and power: for thou hast created all
> things, and for thy pleasure they are and were
> created. -- Rev 4:11**

The number of the angels can be described as both
established and innumerable. It is settled because direct
creation has ceased (Gen 2:1-3) and angels do not
procreate (Mat 22:30). It is immeasurable because it is
implied that there is one angel for each man (Mat 18:10),
angels are associated with stars (Rev 1:20), of which it is
always suggested that they are innumerable (Gen 15:5,
22:17; Deu 1:10), although God does know their number
(Ps 147:4); and finally, the Bible indicates so. The Lord
Jesus Christ maintained that he could get the assistance
of **"twelve legions of angels"** (Mat 26:53). Although
angels are described as **"a multitude"** (Luke 1:13), and
"an innumerable company" (Heb 12:22), when numbered, they are in the thousands:

> **The chariots of God are twenty thousand, even
> thousands of angels: the Lord is among them,
> as in Sinai, in the holy place. -- Psa 68:17**

> **And I beheld, and I heard the voice of many angels round about the throne and the beasts and the elders: and the number of them was ten thousand times ten thousand, and thousands of thousands; -- Rev 5:11**

The number of angels was fixed at 301,655,722 in the fourteenth century,[14] but as this was arrived at by sophistry, we move on.

When angels do appear on the earth, it is usually only a single angel at a time. Twice it is revealed they came in pairs (Gen 19:1; John 12:12), twice we are informed of a group of four angels (Rev 7:1, 9:14), and three times we find a company of seven angels:

> **The mystery of the seven stars which thou sawest in my right hand, and the seven golden candlesticks. The seven stars are the angels of the seven churches: and the seven candlesticks which thou sawest are the seven churches. -- Rev 1:20**

> **And I saw the seven angels which stood before God; and to them were given seven trumpets. -- Rev 8:2**

> **And I saw another sign in heaven, great and marvellous, seven angels having the seven last plagues; for in them is filled up the wrath of God. -- Rev 15:1**

Although the only other mention of an angel standing before God is that of Gabriel (Luke 1:19), the pseudepigraphical, apocalyptic book of Enoch has only four angels that stand before God[15] and turns one archangel (1 Th 4:16) into seven.[16]

The organization of angels is a simple one, but it has suffered from countless misconceptions. Of all the angels mentioned in the Bible, only two are named: Gabriel and Michael. Gabriel—which means man of God or strength of God—and Michael—which means one who is like God—were made of fire and snow respectively, at least according to ancient pagan superstition.[17] Besides Gabriel and Michael, two angels named Raphael, and Uriel are also supposed to stand before God.[18] Raphael was conjectured to be the guardian of human spirits,[19] while Uriel was made the guardian of the underworld.[20] In addition to these, ancient Jewish theorists also included Phanuel, Raguel, Saraquel, Remiel, Sandalphon, and Ridya as among the angels of God,[21] headed up by the supreme angel Metatron.[22]

The only distinction of angels revealed in the Bible (excepting the angel of the Lord) is the designation of Michael alone as **"the archangel"** (1 Th 4:16, Jude 9), which designation *does not* appear frequently.[23] He is also, as pertaining to the nation of Israel, referred to as **"your prince"** (Dan 10:21) and **"the great prince which standeth for the children of thy people"** (Dan 12:1). This is a far cry from the three hierarchies and nine orders of angels discussed by Aquinas which he got from the *Celestial Hierarchy* of Dionysius,[24] which Calvin recognized as "mere babbling"[25] and even Barth called "one of the greatest frauds in Church History."[26] This in turn was influenced by the bogus ranks of Jerome and Ambrose.[27] Throughout history, angels have been assigned to various numbers of ranks or orders, with seven, nine, and twelve being popular arrangements.[28]

Of all the biblical terms that are applied to angels, only four can be scripturally proved. That they are called **"sons of God"** (Job 1:6, 2:1, 38:7) and **"stars"** (Rev 1:20) is acknowledged by all and will be discussed subsequently. The angels are also termed the **"host"** of God:

> **And Jacob went on his way, and the angels of God met him. And when Jacob saw them, he said, This is God's host: and he called the name of that place Mahanaim. -- Gen 32:1-2**

> **And suddenly there was with the angel a multitude of the heavenly host praising God, and saying, Glory to God in the highest, and on earth peace, good will toward men. And it came to pass, as the angels were gone away from them into heaven, the shepherds said one to**

> **another, Let us now go even unto Bethlehem,
> and see this thing which is come to pass, which
> the Lord hath made known unto us. -- Luke
> 2:13-15**

The angels have a captain: **"the captain of the Lord's
host"** (Josh 5:15). The term *host* is also applied in a
general fashion to the ministers of God, which may or
may not be limited to the angels:

> **Bless the LORD, ye his angels, that excel in
> strength, that do his commandments, hearken-
> ing unto the voice of his word. Bless ye the
> LORD, all ye his hosts; ye ministers of his, that
> do his pleasure. -- Psa 103:20-21**

On 245 occasions in the Bible, God is titled the **"Lord of
hosts."** This brings us back to Michael, who, although a
"prince," is nevertheless **"one of the chief princes"**
(Dan 10:13). The only other princes mentioned are the
"prince of the kingdom of Persia" (Dan 10:13) and
the **"prince of Grecia"** (Dan 10:20).

This introduces an unseen spirit world over which
God (Psa 103:19) and the Devil (Mat 12:26) rule. The
point being that, although there are various beings
mentioned in this spirit world, they are not all angels.
Angels are angels. The cherubim are four in number
(Ezek 1:5), have four wings (Ezek 1:6), and God dwells
between them (Isa 37:16), yet they are frequently and
erroneously denominated as angels.[29] Likewise the
seraphim, who not only are *not* mentioned frequently[30]
(they are cited only once), and are described in the Bible
as having six wings and standing above the throne of
God (Isa 6:2), are incorrectly designated as angels[31] and
sometimes the highest angels.[32] This is one place where
the false concept of angels having wings comes from.
Although Satan was originally a cherub (Ezek 28:14),
and can only transform himself into **"an angel of light"**
(2 Cor 11:14), he also is mistakenly called an angel,[33]
usually the highest angel,[34] and a son of God,[35] made in
God's image.[36]   Other spiritual beings that are typical
labeled angels are **"watchers"** (Dan 4:17),[37] **"sons of**

the mighty" (Psa 89:6),[38] "horses and chariots of fire" (2 Kings 6:17),[39] "holy ones" (Dan 4:17),[40] the "four beasts" (Rev 4:6),[41] and the "assembly of the saints" (Psa 89:7).[42] These designations are commonly applied to what is termed good angels; other descriptions of spirit beings are likewise classified as evil angels, and sometimes as good angels. This would include "thrones" and "dominions" (Col 1:16),[43] "principalities" and "powers" (Eph 3:10),[44] "rulers of the darkness of this world" and "spiritual wickedness in high places" (Eph 6:12),[45] "authority and power" (1 Cor 15:24)[46] and "demons," usually classified as fallen angels.[47] The non-biblical terms "virtues"[48] and "angels of the throne"[49] are even applied to angels. Whatever the origin, nature, work, and destiny of these spiritual beings, in the Bible they are not called angels. Angels are angels.

The abode of the angels, since they continually serve and worship God, is always heaven. They are said to be "in heaven" (Mat 18:10, 22:30; Rev 14:17) and "of heaven" (Mat 24:36). They fly in and through "midst of heaven" (Rev 8:13, 14:6), and come "from heaven" (Luke 22:43; Gal 1:8; Rev 20:1) to the earth (Gen 28:12) and back to heaven (Luke 2:15). There is one angel, however, who is called after his dwelling place: "the angel of the bottomless pit" (Rev 9:11), and others "cast down to hell" (2 Pet 2:4), "reserved in everlasting chains" (Jude 6) that will be considered succeedingly.

The initial state of the angels, considering the nature of God, and the examples in the account of the creation of the earth (Gen 1:10,12,18,21,25,31),would have had to be good and just. Yet when Satan fell (Isa 14; Ezek 28), some of the angels apparently fell with him, for the Lord Jesus Christ recognized that the devil has his angels:

> Then shall he say also unto them on the left hand, Depart from me, ye cursed, into everlasting fire, prepared for the devil and his angels:
> -- Mat 25:41

These angels of Satan have been conjectured to be one-third of the original angels by making a future event—**"the third part of the stars of heaven"** (Rev 12:4)—angels who fell with Satan.[50] It has also been determined that there were a total of 133,306,668 angels who fell.[51] In addition to Satan's angels who fell before the creation of the earth, there are other angels who have fallen since then:

> **For if God spared not the angels that sinned, but cast them down to hell, and delivered them into chains of darkness, to be reserved unto judgment; -- 2 Pet 2:4**

> **And the angels which kept not their first estate, but left their own habitation, he hath reserved in everlasting chains under darkness unto the judgment of the great day. -- Jude 6**

This explains the **"sons of God"** in Genesis 6:2, and actually, is the only proof that **"sons of God"** (Job 1:6, 2:1, 38:7) is a reference to angels, since Satan's angels are not bound directly (Rev 12:7, 9). The angels **"bound in the great river Euphrates"** (Rev 9:14) are loosed before judgment (Rev 9:15), so it is not plausible that they are related to the **"angels that sinned"** (2 Pet 2:4), **"which kept not their first estate"** (Jude 6). It is apparent that there are two classes of angels, evil angels and good angels, but both angels nevertheless.

The nature of angels

The nature of angels, a subject directly referred to in the Bible (Heb 2:16), encompasses several particulars with varying degrees of information and detail. First and foremost is their spirituality, the essence of their nature. Then there is their constitution, the tangibility of their nature. Next is their psychological and physiological attributes, and finally, their character. There is perhaps here, the nature of angels, more than anywhere else, that the greatest profusion of error exists regarding angels. Therefore, it is of the utmost importance that the

Scripture be strictly adhered to, correcting all delusions and misconceptions of men.

Throughout history it was thought that the angels had ethereal or fiery bodies, but the Bible describes angels as **"spirits"** (Ps 104:4), or more specifically, **"ministering spirits"** (Heb 1:14). This was taught by Jesus Christ (Mat 22:30), and even the Pharisees recognized it (Acts 23:8). They are inferior to Jesus Christ (Heb 1:4), although he **"was made a little lower than the angels for the suffering of death"** (Heb 2:9), but on a higher level than man (Ps 8:5). Therefore, they could not have been "created in the image and likeness of God just as was man."[52] The Bible describes them as **"a flaming fire"** (Psa 104:4). With the ability to appear to men in a dream (Mat 2:19), and the fact that they are immortal (Luke 20:36), angels have on occasion been objects of worship (Col 2:18; Rev 22:8).

Although angels are spiritual in nature, their tangible constitution is such that **"some have entertained angels unawares"** (Heb 13:2). This is because angels, consistent with every passage in which a description is given, are said to be men:

> **Yea, whiles I was speaking in prayer, even the man Gabriel, whom I had seen in the vision at the beginning, being caused to fly swiftly, touched me about the time of the evening oblation. -- Dan 9:21**

> **And he measured the wall thereof, an hundred and forty and four cubits, according to the measure of a man, that is, of the angel. -- Rev 21:17**

After the resurrection of the Lord Jesus Christ there was seen a **"young man"** (Mark 16:55) and **"two men"** (Luke 24:4) in the tomb who were identified as angels:

> **And when they found not his body, they came, saying, that they had also seen a vision of angels, which said that he was alive. -- Luke 24:23**

> **And seeth two angels in white sitting, the one**

> **at the head, and the other at the feet, where the body of Jesus had lain. -- John 20:12**

Mary saw the angel Gabriel as **"him"** (Luke 1:29) and Daniel said he had **"the appearance of a man"** (Dan 10:18). Cornelius had a vision of **"an angel of God"** (Acts 10:3), but later said it was **"a man"** (Acts 10:30). **"Two men"** (Acts 1:10) appeared to the disciples after the ascension of the Lord Jesus Christ. The **"two angels"** (Gen 19:1) who destroyed Sodom and Gomorrah are called **"the men"** (Gen 18:16, 19:5,10,12). The extent to which they appeared to be men can be seen in the response to their coming by the Sodomites:

> **But before they lay down, the men of the city, even the men of Sodom, compassed the house round, both old and young, all the people from every quarter: And they called unto Lot, and said unto him, Where are the men which came in to thee this night? bring them out unto us, that we may know them. -- Gen 19:4-5**

Yet it is persistently maintained that angels are sexless,[53] only "sometimes described as men,"[54] "generally take on the form of a man"[55] or usually "appear as males,"[56] and that they can be "non-human in appearance."[57] To make things worse, the women who **"had wings like the wings of a stork"** (Zec 5:9) are sometimes recognized as angels.[58] This is another place where the spurious notion of angels having wings comes from, although it is trumpeted over and over again.[59]

Although angels do not have **"flesh and blood"** (Heb 2:14), they have **"hands"** (Rev 8:4), and a face (Acts 6:15). They spoke to men (Zec 2:3; Rev 21:9), were understood, and spoke to God as well (Rev 16:5). They also have some sort of language all their own (1 Cor 10:1). The manna eaten by the children of Israel is identified as **"angels food"** (Psa 78:25). When angels do appear, their garments are always described in similar terms:

> **And entering into the sepulchre, they saw a young man sitting on the right side, clothed in**

a long white garment; and they were affrighted. -- Mark 16:5

And seeth two angels in white sitting, the one at the head, and the other at the feet, where the body of Jesus had lain. -- John 20:12

And while they looked stedfastly toward heaven as he went up, behold, two men stood by them in white apparel; -- Acts 1:10

And the seven angels came out of the temple, having the seven plagues, clothed in pure and white linen, and having their breasts girded with golden girdles. -- Rev 15:6

Angels are also said to have **"glory"** (Rev 18:1), although never the halo accepted by some,[60] and their voice was mistaken for **"thunder"** (John 12:29). With this much clear evidence in the Bible, it is incredible that it could still be said that it is "impossible to determine their material objectivity in detail."[61]

The intellectual and emotional faculties of angels are on a high psychological plane. Twice they are associated with wisdom:

Then thine handmaid said, The word of my lord the king shall now be comfortable: for as an angel of God, so is my lord the king to discern good and bad: therefore the LORD thy God will be with thee. -- 2 Sam 14:17

To fetch about this form of speech hath thy servant Joab done this thing: and my lord is wise, according to the wisdom of an angel of God, to know all things that are in the earth. -- 2 Sam 14:20

They have knowledge of the prayers of men (Luke 1:13) and future events (Rev 17:1), but not absolutely (Mat 24:36). They also are interested in spiritual things (1 Pet 1:12).

The physiological abilities of the angels are extraordinary. Twice we read that angels are **"mighty"** (2 Thes 1:7; Rev 18:21) and one time that they are **"strong"** (Rev 5:2). The angels are said to **"excel in strength"**

(Ps 103:20), have **"great power"** (Rev 18:1), and be **"greater in power and might"** (2 Pet 2:11) than men. Twice it is indicated that angels can fly (Rev 8:13, 14:6), although, as we have seen, they do not have wings; nor would they need them, considering that angels can go to the sun without them (Rev 19:17). One angel will bind Satan for **"a thousand years, And cast him into the bottomless pit"** (Rev 20:1-2). A single angel can also speak from the heavens and be heard on the earth (Rev 8:13, 19:17). Angels can also exercise power over the elements (Rev 7:1) and smite men with blindness (Gen 19:11).

The exceptional character of angels is also readily apparent. Angels were thought to be good and virtuous:

> **And Achish answered and said to David, I know that thou art good in my sight, as an angel of God: notwithstanding the princes of the Philistines have said, He shall not go up with us to the battle. -- 1 Sam 29:9**

> **And he hath slandered thy servant unto my lord the king; but my lord the king is as an angel of God: do therefore what is good in thine eyes. -- 2 Sam 19:27**

Although denominated evil when serving God to the detriment of men (Ps 78:49), angels, excepting those that are fallen (2 Pet 2:4; Jude 6), and those that are associated with Satan (Mat 25:41; Rev 12:7,9), are termed **"elect"** (1 Tim 5:21), **"holy"** (Mat 25:31; Acts 10:22; Rev 14:10), and are associated with light (2 Cor 11:14). This is not to say that they are perfect like God, for even **"his angels he charged with folly"** (Job 4:18), but they do obey God (Psa 103:20), worship him (Rev 5:11-12), and direct men to worship him (Rev 22:9). Their character is so distinguished that men attempted to make them objects of worship (Col 2:18; Rev 22:8).

The work of angels

The work of angels involves much more than simply

being the messengers they are often described as. When we survey the work of angels, we have in mind their activities and duties, both to particular individuals and groups, as well as their operations in general. Their dealings with specific men and groups usually encompasses the work of individual angel or a small number of them while their general occupation routinely includes the aggregate number of all the angels. The work of the angels in general is maintained at all times and is typically related to God; the functions of one or more angels in particular vary in time and are customarily appertain to men.

The totality of the angels, and all men for that matter, have as their supreme duty the worship and praise of God:

> **And suddenly there was with the angel a multitude of the heavenly host praising God, and saying, -- Luke 2:13**

> **And I beheld, and I heard the voice of many angels round about the throne and the beasts and the elders: and the number of them was ten thousand times ten thousand, and thousands of thousands; Saying with a loud voice, Worthy is the Lamb that was slain to receive power, and riches, and wisdom, and strength, and honour, and glory, and blessing. -- Rev 5:11-12**

> **And all the angels stood round about the throne, and about the elders and the four beasts, and fell before the throne on their faces, and worshipped God, -- Rev 7:11**

> **Praise ye him, all his angels: praise ye him, all his hosts. -- Psa 148:2**

> **And again, when he bringeth in the firstbegotten into the world, he saith, And let all the angels of God worship him. -- Heb 1:6**

Angels are God's **"ministers"** (Psa 104:4), doing **"his commandments, hearkening unto the voice of his word"** (Psa 103:20), and are aware of men's activities:

> **Likewise, I say unto you, there is joy in the presence of the angels of God over one sinner that repenteth. -- Luke 15:10**

> **For I think that God hath set forth us the apostles last, as it were appointed to death: for we are made a spectacle unto the world, and to angels, and to men. -- 1 Cor 4:9**

> **I charge thee before God, and the Lord Jesus Christ, and the elect angels, that thou observe these things without preferring one before another, doing nothing by partiality. -- 1 Tim 5:21**

They even desire to look further into spiritual things (1 Pet 1:12). It also appears that children do have a guardian angel (Mat 18:10), but certainly not like described in the pseudepigraphal Apocalypse of Paul.[62] On occasion, and perhaps always, they escort the righteous dead from the earth (Luke 16:22).

The angels are also used to bear witness to certain events:

> **Also I say unto you, Whosoever shall confess me before men, him shall the Son of man also confess before the angels of God: But he that denieth me before men shall be denied before the angels of God. -- Luke 12:8-9**

> **He that overcometh, the same shall be clothed in white raiment; and I will not blot out his name out of the book of life, but I will confess his name before my Father, and before his angels. -- Rev 3:5**

> **The same shall drink of the wine of the wrath of God, which is poured out without mixture into the cup of his indignation; and he shall be tormented with fire and brimstone in the presence of the holy angels, and in the presence of the Lamb: -- Rev 14:10**

There is also to be considered the work of certain angels in particular. This can be divided into three categories, each of which displays the relationship of specific angels to God, Jesus Christ, and man. In relation

to God we find one angel, Gabriel (Luke 1:19), and a
group of seven (Rev 8:2), that stand before God. One
angel is said to have **"the seal of the living God"** (Rev
7:2). Some angels will have the privilege of addressing
God:

> **And I heard the angel of the waters say, Thou
> art righteous, O Lord, which art, and wast, and
> shalt be, because thou hast judged thus. -- Rev
> 16:5**

> **And I heard another out of the altar say, Even
> so, Lord God Almighty, true and righteous are
> thy judgments. -- Rev 16:7**

The angels were and are intrinsically connected with
the ministry of Jesus Christ. The angel Gabriel heralded
his birth (Luke 1:26-38). An angel instructed Joseph
concerning the Lord after his birth (Mat 2:19). During
his ministry, he was **"seen of angels"** (1 Tim 3:16) and
was tended to by them, both actually (Mat 4:11; Luke
22:43; John 1:51) and potentially (Mat 26:53). Another
angel signified and testified on his behalf (Rev 1:1,
22:16), still another revealed his resurrection (Luke
24:4-6). The angels also figure prominently at his return:

> **For the Son of man shall come in the glory of
> his Father with his angels; and then he shall
> reward every man according to his works. --
> Mat 16:27**

> **When the Son of man shall come in his glory,
> and all the holy angels with him, then shall he
> sit upon the throne of his glory: -- Mat 25:31**

> **And to you who are troubled rest with us,
> when the Lord Jesus shall be revealed from
> heaven with his mighty angels, -- 2 Th 1:7**

An angel or angels also intervened in the affairs of
men at various times. The fact that angels were said to
have spoke to men was readily accepted throughout the
Bible:

> **He said unto him, I am a prophet also as thou
> art; and an angel spake unto me by the word of**

the LORD, saying, Bring him back with thee
into thine house, that he may eat bread and
drink water. But he lied unto him. -- 1 Ki 13:18

The people therefore, that stood by, and heard
it, said that it thundered: others said, An angel
spake to him. -- John 12:29

And there arose a great cry: and the scribes
that were of the Pharisees' part arose, and
strove, saying, We find no evil in this man: but
if a spirit or an angel hath spoken to him, let us
not fight against God. -- Acts 23:9

Two angels brought Lot out of Sodom and destroyed the
city (Gen 19:15). The **"angels of God"** met Jacob (Gen
32:1). Angels were involved with the giving of the law:

Who have received the law by the disposition of
angels, and have not kept it. -- Acts 7:53

Wherefore then serveth the law? It was added
because of transgressions, till the seed should
come to whom the promise was made; and it
was ordained by angels in the hand of a
mediator. -- Gal 3:19

For if the word spoken by angels was stedfast,
and every transgression and disobedience received a just recompense of reward; -- Heb 2:2

Angels render either good (Psa 91:11) or evil (Psa 78:49)
to individuals depending on what they deserve. A single
angel conversed with Zechariah (Zec 1:9), another
"troubled the water" (John 5:4) at the pool of
Bethesda, and another warned Cornelius (Acts 10:3,22).
The angel Gabriel announced the birth of John the
Baptist (Luke 1:11-20). The future will witness a revival
in the work of the angels. The judgments in the
Tribulation will be transmitted by angels (Rev 8:5-12,
9:1,13-15, 11:15, 14:15-19, 15:1), during which time ten
angels will speak (Rev 5:2, 7:2, 8:13, 14:6-7,8,9,15,18,
18:21, 19:17). God's angels will someday fight against
Satan's angels (Rev 12:7) and one angel will bind Satan
(Rev 20:1-2). And finally, twelve angels will be at the
gates of new Jerusalem (Rev 21:12).

The destiny of angels

There is not much information in the Bible regarding the ultimate destiny of angels for the simple reason that the majority of them have remained harmonious throughout their protracted existence. There are two classes of angels, however, that await a bitter end. The first are those angels that are associated with the devil as **"his angels"** (Mat 25:41; Rev 12:7,9). There is coming a day in the future when "star wars" will literally take place:

> **And there was war in heaven: Michael and his angels fought against the dragon; and the dragon fought and his angels, -- Rev 12:7**

> **And the great dragon was cast out, that old serpent, called the Devil, and Satan, which deceiveth the whole world: he was cast out into the earth, and his angels were cast out with him. -- Rev 12:9**

If angels are stars (Rev 1:20), then another verse is also applicable:

> **And his tail drew the third part of the stars of heaven, and did cast them to the earth: and the dragon stood before the woman which was ready to be delivered, for to devour her child as soon as it was born. -- Rev 12:4**

As previously mentioned, these angels will literally fall in the future; this is not a reference to immediately after Genesis 1:1. After these events have transpired, the final destiny for these angels is the same as for the devil himself:

> **Then shall he say also unto them on the left hand, Depart from me, ye cursed, into everlasting fire, prepared for the devil and his angels: -- Mat 25:41**

The second group of angels awaiting their final dwelling place have not just already fallen, they are secured:

> **For if God spared not the angels that sinned,**

> **but cast them down to hell, and delivered them into chains of darkness, to be reserved unto judgment; -- 2 Pet 2:4**

> **And the angels which kept not their first estate, but left their own habitation, he hath reserved in everlasting chains under darkness unto the judgment of the great day. -- Jude 1:6**

This explains the peculiar reference by Paul that Christians shall in the future judge angels:

> **Know ye not that we shall judge angels? how much more things that pertain to this life? -- 1 Cor 6:3**

It should be noted that hell was originally **"prepared for the devil and his angels"** (Mat 25:41), any sinner who goes there will be an eternal unwelcome prisoner.

As one can plainly see, the angels of God occupy an important place in the Scripture. It is certainly not their insignificance that has fostered the labyrinth of misconception and delusion concerning them. As prominent as angels are, there is one angel in the Bible that commands much greater examination due to the preeminent place given him: the angel of the Lord.

CHAPTER THREE

THE ANGEL OF THE LORD

Although the angel of the Lord is mentioned in the Bible fifty-nine times in fifty-eight verses, appearing in eleven books of the Old Testament and three of the New, not every account or every verse denotes a separate and distinct appearance. Neither is every angel termed the angel of the Lord really *the* angel of the Lord. This connotation of an angel is the most frequent one appearing in the Bible, but there are other manifestations of the angel of the Lord that do not refer to him exactly in this manner. There are twenty-one distinct presentations of the angel of the Lord, and besides these instances in which the angel of the Lord is mentioned as doing or saying something, we have five allusions to the angel of the Lord, parallel accounts to two episodes in Kings, places where the angel of the Lord is called an angel of the Lord, those locales where the angel of the Lord is designated as an angel or by some other description, and some overlap between the categories. Since it is the most common, we begin with those references that refer directly to some action of the angel of the Lord.

The angel of the Lord in Genesis

The first occurrence of the angel of the Lord in the Bible is also the first reference to an angel. Sarah persuaded Abraham to have a child by her maid Hagar. When Hagar conceived and **"her mistress was despised in her eyes"** (Gen 16:4), she fled due to the hard treatment she received. In this account we find four verses that mention the angel of the Lord:

> **And the angel of the LORD found her by a**
> **fountain of water in the wilderness, by the**
> **fountain in the way to Shur. And he said,**
> **Hagar, Sarai's maid, whence camest thou? and**
> **whither wilt thou go? And she said, I flee from**
> **the face of my mistress Sarai. And the angel of**
> **the LORD said unto her, Return to thy mis-**
> **tress, and submit thyself under her hands. And**
> **the angel of the LORD said unto her, I will**
> **multiply thy seed exceedingly, that it shall not**
> **be numbered for multitude. And the angel of**
> **the LORD said unto her, Behold, thou art with**
> **child, and shalt bear a son, and shalt call his**
> **name Ishmael; because the LORD hath heard**
> **thy affliction. And he will be a wild man; his**
> **hand will be against every man, and every**
> **man's hand against him; and he shall dwell in**
> **the presence of all his brethren. -- Gen 16:7-12**

Three times we are here told that the angel of the Lord spoke directly to Hagar, issuing instruction, blessing, and forecast. Although it is assumed that the angel of the Lord appeared to her when speaking, it is not clearly stated.

The next report of the angel of the Lord is when Abraham attempted to offer his son Isaac **"for a burnt offering"** (Gen 22:2). After journeying to the appointed place, Abraham bound his son and **"laid him on the altar upon the wood"** (Gen 22:10). As he sought to slay him, the angel of the Lord intervened:

> **And the angel of the LORD called unto him out**
> **of heaven, and said, Abraham, Abraham: and**
> **he said, Here am I. And he said, Lay not thine**
> **hand upon the lad, neither do thou any thing**
> **unto him: for now I know that thou fearest**
> **God, seeing thou hast not withheld thy son,**
> **thine only son from me. And Abraham lifted up**
> **his eyes, and looked, and behold behind him a**
> **ram caught in a thicket by his horns: and**
> **Abraham went and took the ram, and offered**
> **him up for a burnt offering in the stead of his**
> **son. And Abraham called the name of that**

> place Jehovahjireh: as it is said to this day, In
> the mount of the LORD it shall be seen. And
> the angel of the LORD called unto Abraham
> out of heaven the second time, And said, By
> myself have I sworn, saith the LORD, for
> because thou hast done this thing, and hast not
> withheld thy son, thine only son: That in
> blessing I will bless thee, and in multiplying I
> will multiply thy seed as the stars of the
> heaven, and as the sand which is upon the sea
> shore; and thy seed shall possess the gate of his
> enemies; And in thy seed shall all the nations
> of the earth be blessed; because thou hast
> obeyed my voice. -- Gen 22:11-18

Here the angel of the Lord undeniably appears to no one:
he twice speaks from heaven. First, to rescue Isaac, and
second, to offer reward and blessing to Abraham.

The angel of the Lord in Exodus

The only portrait given in the book of Exodus of the
angel of the Lord concerns his appearance to Moses at
the burning bush. Moses was tending his flock **"and
came to the mountain of God"** (Exo 3:1) where he
subsequently had an encounter that was to change his
life forever:

> And the angel of the LORD appeared unto him
> in a flame of fire out of the midst of a bush: and
> he looked, and, behold, the bush burned with
> fire, and the bush was not consumed. And
> Moses said, I will now turn aside, and see this
> great sight, why the bush is not burnt. And
> when the LORD saw that he turned aside to
> see, God called unto him out of the midst of the
> bush, and said, Moses, Moses. And he said,
> Here am I. And he said, Draw not nigh hither:
> put off thy shoes from off thy feet, for the place
> whereon thou standest is holy ground. -- Exo
> 3:2-5

Unlike the previous two accounts, this was certainly
both an appearance of the angel of the Lord as well as a
verbal address.

The angel of the Lord in Numbers

Though the angel of the Lord is only presented on one occasion in the book of Numbers, he is cited ten times in as many verses. This is the greatest number of references to the angel of the Lord in any one context. The occasion was Balaam **"going with the princes of Moab"** (Num 22:21), after originally being told: **"thou shalt not go with them"** (Num 22:12):

> And God's anger was kindled because he went: and the angel of the LORD stood in the way for an adversary against him. Now he was riding upon his ass, and his two servants were with him. And the ass saw the angel of the LORD standing in the way, and his sword drawn in his hand: and the ass turned aside out of the way, and went into the field: and Balaam smote the ass, to turn her into the way. But the angel of the LORD stood in a path of the vineyards, a wall being on this side, and a wall on that side. And when the ass saw the angel of the LORD, she thrust herself unto the wall, and crushed Balaam's foot against the wall: and he smote her again. And the angel of the LORD went further, and stood in a narrow place, where was no way to turn either to the right hand or to the left. And when the ass saw the angel of the LORD, she fell down under Balaam: and Balaam's anger was kindled, and he smote the ass with a staff. And the LORD opened the mouth of the ass, and she said unto Balaam, What have I done unto thee, that thou hast smitten me these three times? And Balaam said unto the ass, Because thou hast mocked me: I would there were a sword in mine hand, for now would I kill thee. And the ass said unto Balaam, Am not I thine ass, upon which thou hast ridden ever since I was thine unto this day? was I ever wont to do so unto thee? And he said, Nay. Then the LORD opened the eyes of Balaam, and he saw the angel of the LORD standing in the way, and his sword drawn in his hand: and he bowed down his head, and fell flat on his face. And the angel of the LORD said

> unto him, Wherefore hast thou smitten thine
> ass these three times? behold, I went out to
> withstand thee, because thy way is perverse
> before me: And the ass saw me, and turned
> from me these three times: unless she had
> turned from me, surely now also I had slain
> thee, and saved her alive. And Balaam said
> unto the angel of the LORD, I have sinned; for I
> knew not that thou stoodest in the way against
> me: now therefore, if it displease thee, I will
> get me back again. And the angel of the LORD
> said unto Balaam, Go with the men: but only
> the word that I shall speak unto thee, that thou
> shalt speak. So Balaam went with the princes
> of Balak. -- Num 22:22-35

Although mentioned ten times, only twice does the angel
of the Lord say anything: once a question and the other
time a command. This is also the first place where the
angel of the Lord does something besides merely speak.

The angel of the Lord in Judges

The book of Judges chronicles three separate accounts of the angel of the Lord in fifteen verses,
mentioning the angel of the Lord nineteen times. This is
more than is found in any other book of the Bible. The
first is his instruction to the children of Israel, where he
is mentioned twice:

> And an angel of the LORD came up from Gilgal
> to Bochim, and said, I made you to go up out of
> Egypt, and have brought you unto the land
> which I sware unto your fathers; and I said, I
> will never break my covenant with you. And ye
> shall make no league with the inhabitants of
> this land; ye shall throw down their altars: but
> ye have not obeyed my voice: why have ye done
> this? Wherefore I also said, I will not drive
> them out from before you; but they shall be as
> thorns in your sides, and their gods shall be a
> snare unto you. And it came to pass, when the
> angel of the LORD spake these words unto all
> the children of Israel, that the people lifted up
> their voice, and wept. -- Judg 2:1-4

Apparently, the children of Israel had an unseen visitor while they were in Gilgal, and since the angel of the Lord physically removed from one city to another, he obviously spoke to them in person and not just from heaven. This is the only time the angel of the Lord appears to a group instead of one or two individuals. It should also be noticed that **"an angel of the Lord"** (Judg 2:1) is here identified as **"the angel of the Lord"** (Judg 2:4).

The second report of the angel of the Lord involves his appearance to Gideon:

> **And there came an angel of the LORD, and sat under an oak which was in Ophrah, that pertained unto Joash the Abiezrite: and his son Gideon threshed wheat by the winepress, to hide it from the Midianites. And the angel of the LORD appeared unto him, and said unto him, The LORD is with thee, thou mighty man of valour. -- Judg 6:11-12**

This is undeniably another direct appearance of the angel of the Lord. It should also be observed again that the angel of the Lord is referred to as **"an angel of the Lord"** (Judg 6:11). After Gideon **"made ready a kid"** (Judg 6:19) and presented it to the angel of the Lord, he was once again addressed by him:

> **And the angel of God said unto him, Take the flesh and the unleavened cakes, and lay them upon this rock, and pour out the broth. And he did so. Then the angel of the LORD put forth the end of the staff that was in his hand, and touched the flesh and the unleavened cakes; and there rose up fire out of the rock, and consumed the flesh and the unleavened cakes. Then the angel of the LORD departed out of his sight. And when Gideon perceived that he was an angel of the LORD, Gideon said, Alas, O Lord GOD! for because I have seen an angel of the LORD face to face. -- Judg 6:20-22**

Several things are apparent here concerning the angel of the Lord. He is termed both **"the angel of God"** (Judg

6:20) and **"an angel of the Lord"** (Judg 6:22), and he does much more than simply appearing and speaking.

The last mention of the angel of the Lord in Judges concerns his appearance to Manoah and his wife, the parents of Samson. The aggregate of references to the angel of the Lord in this context encompasses eight verses, making this the second largest number of allusions to the angel of the Lord in any one setting. The occasion for this appearance was the fact that Manoah's wife was barren:

> **And the angel of the LORD appeared unto the woman, and said unto her, Behold now, thou art barren, and bearest not: but thou shalt conceive, and bear a son. -- Judg 13:3**

After materializing to Manoah's wife the second time, she went and got her husband:

> **And the angel of the LORD said unto Manoah, Of all that I said unto the woman let her beware. She may not eat of any thing that cometh of the vine, neither let her drink wine or strong drink, nor eat any unclean thing: all that I commanded her let her observe. And Manoah said unto the angel of the LORD, I pray thee, let us detain thee, until we shall have made ready a kid for thee. And the angel of the LORD said unto Manoah, Though thou detain me, I will not eat of thy bread: and if thou wilt offer a burnt offering, thou must offer it unto the LORD. For Manoah knew not that he was an angel of the LORD. And Manoah said unto the angel of the LORD, What is thy name, that when thy sayings come to pass we may do thee honour? And the angel of the LORD said unto him, Why askest thou thus after my name, seeing it is secret? So Manoah took a kid with a meat offering, and offered it upon a rock unto the LORD: and the angel did wonderously; and Manoah and his wife looked on. For it came to pass, when the flame went up toward heaven from off the altar, that the angel of the LORD ascended in the flame of the altar. And Manoah and his wife looked on it, and fell on their faces**

> **to the ground. But the angel of the LORD did
> no more appear to Manoah and to his wife.
> Then Manoah knew that he was an angel of the
> LORD. -- Judg 13:13-21**

The supernatural character of the angel of the Lord is
beginning to become more readily apparent. There are
also four designations given in the context for the angel
of the Lord: **"a man of God"** (Judg 13:6), **"an angel of
God"** (Judg 13:6), **"the angel of God"** (Judg 13:9), **"an
angel of the Lord"** (Judg 13:16).

The angel of the Lord in Samuel

The eighth account of the angel of the Lord interven-
ing in the affairs of men is the only one in 2 Samuel. The
occasion was the sin of David in numbering the people:

> **So the LORD sent a pestilence upon Israel
> from the morning even to the time appointed:
> and there died of the people from Dan even to
> Beersheba seventy thousand men. And when
> the angel stretched out his hand upon Jerusa-
> lem to destroy it, the LORD repented him of
> the evil, and said to the angel that destroyed
> the people, It is enough: stay now thine hand.
> And the angel of the LORD was by the thresh-
> ingplace of Araunah the Jebusite. And David
> spake unto the LORD when he saw the angel
> that smote the people, and said, Lo, I have
> sinned, and I have done wickedly: but these
> sheep, what have they done? let thine hand, I
> pray thee, be against me, and against my
> father's house. -- 2 Sam 24:15-17**

This the most active pursuit undertaken by the angel of
the Lord thus far. No record of the angel speaking is
intimated. Mentioned only once in the books of Samuel,
the narrative here about the angel of the Lord is
repeated in Chronicles with more detail.

The angel of the Lord in Kings

There are three distinct narratives of the angel of the

Lord in the books of 1 and 2 Kings, two of them involving the prophet Elijah. The first happened after Elijah fled from Jezebel and **"sat down under a juniper tree"** (1 Kings 19:4):

> **And as he lay and slept under a juniper tree, behold, then an angel touched him, and said unto him, Arise and eat. And he looked, and, behold, there was a cake baken on the coals, and a cruse of water at his head. And he did eat and drink, and laid him down again. And the angel of the LORD came again the second time, and touched him, and said, Arise and eat; because the journey is too great for thee. And he arose, and did eat and drink, and went in the strength of that meat forty days and forty nights unto Horeb the mount of God. -- 1 Ki 19:5-8**

The angel of the Lord is here first referred to as simply **"an angel"** (1 Kings 19:5). The angel both appears and speaks with Elijah.

The second event embodying Elijah took place upon the sickness of king Ahaziah, who inquired **"of Baalzebub the god of Ekron"** (2 Kings 1:2) instead of the Lord God:

> **But the angel of the LORD said to Elijah the Tishbite, Arise, go up to meet the messengers of the king of Samaria, and say unto them, Is it not because there is not a God in Israel, that ye go to inquire of Baalzebub the god of Ekron? -- 2 Ki 1:3**

After the king sent two captains with fifty men each to get Elijah, only to have had fire come **"down from heaven, and burnt up the two captains of the former fifties with their fifties"** (2 Kings 1:14), the angel of the Lord enlightened Elijah as to his reaction to a third captain with fifty men:

> **And the angel of the LORD said unto Elijah, Go down with him: be not afraid of him. And he arose, and went down with him unto the king. -- 2 Ki 1:15**

It is not mentioned the manner in which the angel of the Lord spoke to Elijah, whether a discourse from heaven or direct appearance.

The last reference to the angel of the Lord in Kings comprises neither speaking nor any lasting appearance:

> **And it came to pass that night, that the angel of the LORD went out, and smote in the camp of the Assyrians an hundred fourscore and five thousand: and when they arose early in the morning, behold, they were all dead corpses. -- 2 Ki 19:35**

Whether the dead Assyrians saw the angel of the Lord before their demise is not evident. In any case, this is the most vehement endeavor undertaken by the angel of the Lord anywhere in the Bible.

The angel of the Lord in Zechariah

The last book in the Old Testament contains more references to angels than any other, and introduces the angel of the Lord on two occasions. These transpire during a revelation of God to the prophet Zechariah. The first is Zechariah's inaugural vision:

> **And they answered the angel of the LORD that stood among the myrtle trees, and said, We have walked to and fro through the earth, and, behold, all the earth sitteth still, and is at rest. Then the angel of the LORD answered and said, O LORD of hosts, how long wilt thou not have mercy on Jerusalem and on the cities of Judah, against which thou hast had indignation these threescore and ten years? -- Zec 1:11-12**

Like the case of the burning bush, this was certainly both an appearance and a verbal address. It should also be noted that the angel of the Lord is here in the context called **"a man"** (Zec 1:8).

The second occurrence of the angel of the Lord in Zechariah involves the most characters in context with the angel of the Lord than anyplace else in Scripture: the Lord of hosts, the angel of the Lord, Joshua the high priest, Satan, and Zechariah:

> **And he showed me Joshua the high priest standing before the angel of the LORD, and Satan standing at his right hand to resist him. And the LORD said unto Satan, The LORD rebuke thee, O Satan; even the LORD that hath chosen Jerusalem rebuke thee: is not this a brand plucked out of the fire? Now Joshua was clothed with filthy garments, and stood before the angel. And he answered and spake unto those that stood before him, saying, Take away the filthy garments from him. And unto him he said, Behold, I have caused thine iniquity to pass from thee, and I will clothe thee with change of raiment. And I said, Let them set a fair mitre upon his head. So they set a fair mitre upon his head, and clothed him with garments. And the angel of the LORD stood by. And the angel of the LORD protested unto Joshua, saying, Thus saith the LORD of hosts; If thou wilt walk in my ways, and if thou wilt keep my charge, then thou shalt also judge my house, and shalt also keep my courts, and I will give thee places to walk among these that stand by. -- Zec 3:1-7**

The angel of the Lord in Matthew

There are three accounts of the angel of the Lord in Matthew, two of which involve appearances to Joseph in dreams. Joseph thus becomes only the fourth person, after Manoah's wife, Elijah, and Zechariah, to have more than one encounter with the angel of the Lord:

> **But while he thought on these things, behold, the angel of the Lord appeared unto him in a dream, saying, Joseph, thou son of David, fear not to take unto thee Mary thy wife: for that which is conceived in her is of the Holy Ghost. And she shall bring forth a son, and thou shalt call his name JESUS: for he shall save his people from their sins. Now all this was done,**

that it might be fulfilled which was spoken of the Lord by the prophet, saying, Behold, a virgin shall be with child, and shall bring forth a son, and they shall call his name Emmanuel, which being interpreted is, God with us. Then Joseph being raised from sleep did as the angel of the Lord had bidden him, and took unto him his wife: -- Mat 1:20-24

And when they were departed, behold, the angel of the Lord appeareth to Joseph in a dream, saying, Arise, and take the young child and his mother, and flee into Egypt, and be thou there until I bring thee word: for Herod will seek the young child to destroy him. When he arose, he took the young child and his mother by night, and departed into Egypt: And was there until the death of Herod: that it might be fulfilled which was spoken of the Lord by the prophet, saying, Out of Egypt have I called my son. -- Mat 2:13-15

The last reference to the angel of the Lord in Matthew took place after the resurrection:

And, behold, there was a great earthquake: for the angel of the Lord descended from heaven, and came and rolled back the stone from the door, and sat upon it. -- Mat 28:2

The Lord was already out of the tomb, the angel had to move the stone so people could **"see the place where the Lord lay"** (Mat 28:6).

The angel of the Lord in Luke

The Gospel of Luke contributes one account of the angel of the Lord. This is the familiar appearance to the shepherds at the human birth of the Lord Jesus Christ:

And, lo, the angel of the Lord came upon them, and the glory of the Lord shone round about them: and they were sore afraid. And the angel said unto them, Fear not: for, behold, I bring you good tidings of great joy, which shall be to all people. For unto you is born this day in the city of David a Saviour, which is Christ the

> **Lord. And this shall be a sign unto you; Ye shall find the babe wrapped in swaddling clothes, lying in a manger. -- Luke 2:9-12**

The angel of the Lord in Acts

There are four brief narratives of the angel of the Lord in the book of Acts. Two of these are prison breaks:

> **But the angel of the Lord by night opened the prison doors, and brought them forth, and said, Go, stand and speak in the temple to the people all the words of this life. -- Acts 5:19-20**

> **And, behold, the angel of the Lord came upon him, and a light shined in the prison: and he smote Peter on the side, and raised him up, saying, Arise up quickly. And his chains fell off from his hands. -- Acts 12:7**

Although it is obvious in the second account that the angel of the Lord both appeared and spoke, the first is not so perspicuous, but can be readily assumed from the context.

The third mention of the angel of the Lord may or may not have involved a direct appearance:

> **And the angel of the Lord spake unto Philip, saying, Arise, and go toward the south unto the way that goeth down from Jerusalem unto Gaza, which is desert. -- Acts 8:26**

Philip obeyed the command and we are told **"preached unto him Jesus"** (Acts 8:35).

The last occurrence of the angel of the Lord in Acts is also the last mention in the New Testament. King Herod, after killing **"James the brother of John"** (Acts 12:2), made an oration and accepted the people's assertion: **"It is the voice of a god"** (Acts 12:22), with the consequences of:

> **And immediately the angel of the Lord smote him, because he gave not God the glory: and he was eaten of worms, and gave up the ghost. -- Acts 12:23**

This is the third time where the angel of the Lord brings no message but death.

Mentions of the angel of the Lord

In addition to those references to the angel of the Lord where he appears or speaks or does both, there are five instances where he is unpretentiously mentioned and does neither. The first reference where the angel of the Lord is just alluded to is in the book of Judges and occurs within the song of Deborah and Barak after the **"avenging of Israel"** (Judg 5:2):

> **Curse ye Meroz, said the angel of the LORD, curse ye bitterly the inhabitants thereof; because they came not to the help of the LORD, to the help of the LORD against the mighty. -- Judg 5:23**

Though there are three references to the angel of the Lord in the Psalms, these involve a bare mention only, with no record of an appearance, a discourse, or an action, except potentially:

> **The angel of the LORD encampeth round about them that fear him, and delivereth them. -- Psa 34:7**

> **Let them be as chaff before the wind: and let the angel of the LORD chase them. -- Psa 35:5**

> **Let their way be dark and slippery: and let the angel of the LORD persecute them. -- Psa 35:6**

The fifth unassuming reference to the angel of the Lord has a significant millennial application:

> **In that day shall the LORD defend the inhabitants of Jerusalem; and he that is feeble among them at that day shall be as David; and the house of David shall be as God, as the angel of the LORD before them. -- Zec 12:8**

Parallel accounts of the angel of the Lord

Besides the aforementioned allusions to the angel of

the Lord, there are parallel accounts to two passages in Kings. The sole report of the angel of the Lord in Chronicles is just the coinciding narrative of 2 Samuel:

> **Either three years' famine; or three months to be destroyed before thy foes, while that the sword of thine enemies overtaketh thee; or else three days the sword of the LORD, even the pestilence, in the land, and the angel of the LORD destroying throughout all the coasts of Israel. Now therefore advise thyself what word I shall bring again to him that sent me. And David said unto Gad, I am in a great strait: let me fall now into the hand of the LORD; for very great are his mercies: but let me not fall into the hand of man. So the LORD sent pestilence upon Israel: and there fell of Israel seventy thousand men. And God sent an angel unto Jerusalem to destroy it: and as he was destroying, the LORD beheld, and he repented him of the evil, and said to the angel that destroyed, It is enough, stay now thine hand. And the angel of the LORD stood by the threshingfloor of Ornan the Jebusite. And David lifted up his eyes, and saw the angel of the LORD stand between the earth and the heaven, having a drawn sword in his hand stretched out over Jerusalem. Then David and the elders of Israel, who were clothed in sackcloth, fell upon their faces. And David said unto God, Is it not I that commanded the people to be numbered? even I it is that have sinned and done evil indeed; but as for these sheep, what have they done? let thine hand, I pray thee, O LORD my God, be on me, and on my father's house; but not on thy people, that they should be plagued. Then the angel of the LORD commanded Gad to say to David, that David should go up, and set up an altar unto the LORD in the threshingfloor of Ornan the Jebusite. -- 1 Chr 21:12-18**

Once again the angel of the Lord is referred to as **"an angel"** (1 Chr 21:15). Moreover, this account also gives us more detail concerning the work of the angel of the

Lord. For example, here we are told that it was the angel of the Lord who commanded the prophet Gad to instruct David to build **"an altar unto the Lord in the threshingfloor"** (2 Sam 24:18; 1 Chr 21:18). And furthermore, this version alone notifies us that the angel of the Lord spoke anything. We are also informed in the context that David **"was afraid because of the sword of the angel of the Lord"** (1 Chr 21:22).

The second example of a parallel account of the angel of the Lord is almost an exact restatement of 2 Kings 19:35, the slaying of the Assyrians:

> **Then the angel of the LORD went forth, and smote in the camp of the Assyrians a hundred and fourscore and five thousand: and when they arose early in the morning, behold, they were all dead corpses. -- Isa 37:36**

An angel of the Lord

This chapter on the angel of the Lord would not be complete without examining those references where *an angel of the Lord* is reported instead of *the angel of the Lord*. This occurs nine times in eight verses. We gave already seen six instances in five verses where the angel of the Lord was called **"an angel of the Lord"** (Judg 2:1, 6:11, 6:22, 13:16,22) and identified as such in the context. In addition to these, there are three in the New Testament. The first raises two questions:

> **But when Herod was dead, behold, an angel of the Lord appeareth in a dream to Joseph in Egypt, -- Mat 2:19**

Twice previously, Joseph was visited in a dream by the angel of the Lord (Mat 1:20, 2:13), so it could be reasonably assumed that such was the case here. However, even if this were so, we are still left with the inquiry into the identification of the angel of the Lord in the New Testament. Since the angel connected with Christ's birth was Gabriel (Luke 1:26-33) and he is termed **"an angel of the Lord"** (Luke 1:11-19), the angel of the Lord in Matthew could be Gabriel.

In the next account of *an angel of the Lord*, his identity is clearly revealed:

> **And there appeared unto him an angel of the Lord standing on the right side of the altar of incense. -- Luke 1:11**

This angel is positively identified as Gabriel:

> **And the angel answering said unto him, I am Gabriel, that stand in the presence of God; and am sent to speak unto thee, and to show thee these glad tidings. -- Luke 1:19**

The last reference to an angel of the Lord refers back to the familar burning bush narrative in the Old Testament:

> **And when forty years were expired, there appeared to him in the wilderness of mount Sina an angel of the Lord in a flame of fire in a bush. -- Acts 7:30**

The identity of this angel as an angel of the Lord is confirmed in Exodus:

> **And the angel of the LORD appeared unto him in a flame of fire out of the midst of a bush: and he looked, and, behold, the bush burned with fire, and the bush was not consumed. -- Exo 3:2**

Other names for the angel of the Lord

So far all of the references to the angel of the Lord have been by that phrase or the anarthrous use thereof. But there are places in which the angel of the Lord is designated by other angelic terminology. As previously mentioned, many of these fall under the category of referring angels. The others use descriptive terms, the most common of which is the similar expression *the angel of God:*

> **And God heard the voice of the lad; and the angel of God called to Hagar out of heaven, and said unto her, What aileth thee, Hagar? fear**

not; for God hath heard the voice of the lad where he is. -- Gen 21:17

And the angel of God spake unto me in a dream, saying, Jacob: And I said, Here am I. -- Gen 31:11

And the angel of God said unto him, Take the flesh and the unleavened cakes, and lay them upon this rock, and pour out the broth. And he did so. -- Judg 6:20

And the angel of God, which went before the camp of Israel, removed and went behind them; and the pillar of the cloud went from before their face, and stood behind them: -- Exo 14:19

Three times the angel of the Lord is cited by the term *his angel,* relating him in a special way to God:

The LORD God of heaven, which took me from my father's house, and from the land of my kindred, and which spake unto me, and that sware unto me, saying, Unto thy seed will I give this land; he shall send his angel before thee, and thou shalt take a wife unto my son from thence. -- Gen 24:7

Then Nebuchadnezzar spake, and said, Blessed be the God of Shadrach, Meshach, and Abednego, who hath sent his angel, and delivered his servants that trusted in him, and have changed the king's word, and yielded their bodies, that they might not serve nor worship any god, except their own God. -- Dan 3:28

My God hath sent his angel, and hath shut the lions' mouths, that they have not hurt me: forasmuch as before him innocency was found in me; and also before thee, O king, have I done no hurt. -- Dan 6:22

The angel of the Lord is also called a **"mighty angel"** in Revelation. Since he is said to **"stand upon the sea and the earth"** (Rev 10:2), he is twice referred to as the angel who stands **"upon the sea and upon the earth"** (Rev 10:5,8).

Other appellations for the angel of the Lord include *the angel* and *an angel*:

> **The Angel which redeemed me from all evil, bless the lads; and let my name be named on them, and the name of my fathers Abraham and Isaac; and let them grow into a multitude in the midst of the earth. -- Gen 48:16**

> **Behold, I send an Angel before thee, to keep thee in the way, and to bring thee into the place which I have prepared. -- Exo 23:20**

It should be noticed that the angel of the Lord is here emphasized with the capitalization of the word *angel,* hinting that this was no prosaic angel.

These other descriptions of the angel of the Lord are also employed in referencing to a previous or contextual mention of the angel of the Lord. The angel in Exodus 23:20 is referred to four times: twice by *mine angel* and twice by *an angel:*

> **For mine Angel shall go before thee, and bring thee in unto the Amorites, and the Hittites, and the Perizzites, and the Canaanites, the Hivites, and the Jebusites: and I will cut them off. -- Exo 23:23**

> **Therefore now go, lead the people unto the place of which I have spoken unto thee: behold, mine Angel shall go before thee: nevertheless in the day when I visit I will visit their sin upon them. -- Exo 32:34**

> **And I will send an angel before thee; and I will drive out the Canaanite, the Amorite, and the Hittite, and the Perizzite, the Hivite, and the Jebusite: -- Exo 33:2**

> **And when we cried unto the LORD, he heard our voice, and sent an angel, and hath brought us forth out of Egypt: and, behold, we are in Kadesh, a city in the uttermost of thy border: -- Num 20:16**

"His angel" in Genesis 24:7 is synonymously termed in Genesis 24:40. Other referencing descriptions include

"an angel" (1 Kings 19:5; 1 Chr 21:15; 2 Chr 32:21), the
"angel of his presence" (Is 63:9), **"the angel"** (2 Sam
24:16; 1 Chr 21:20,27; Hosea 12:4; Zec 3:3; Rev 10:9, 10,
11:1), **"an angel of God"** (Judg 13:6), **"a man"** (Zec
1:8), and **"a man of God"** (Judg 13:6).

The two concluding alternative names for the angel
of the Lord do not contain the word *angel:*

> **And Jacob was left alone; and there wrestled a
> man with him until the breaking of the day. --
> Gen 32:24**

> **And it came to pass, when Joshua was by
> Jericho, that he lifted up his eyes and looked,
> and, behold, there stood a man over against
> him with his sword drawn in his hand: and
> Joshua went unto him, and said unto him, Art
> thou for us, or for our adversaries? And he
> said, Nay; but as captain of the host of the
> LORD am I now come. And Joshua fell on his
> face to the earth, and did worship, and said
> unto him, What saith my lord unto his servant?
> And the captain of the LORD'S host said unto
> Joshua, Loose thy shoe from off thy foot; for
> the place whereon thou standest is holy. And
> Joshua did so. -- Josh 5:13-15**

The man Jacob wrestled with is identified later:

> **Yea, he had power over the angel, and pre-
> vailed: he wept, and made supplication unto
> him: he found him in Bethel, and there he
> spake with us; -- Hosea 12:4**

That the **"captain of the Lord's host"** is the angel of
the Lord is apparent by an earlier statement made by
the angel of the Lord:

> **And he said, Draw not nigh hither: put off thy
> shoes from off thy feet, for the place whereon
> thou standest is holy ground. -- Exo 3:5**

As a result of all the available scriptural evidence, we
can see that although the angel of the Lord is mentioned
in the Bible fifty-nine times in fifty-eight verses, he is
actually manifested on twenty-seven separate and dis-

tinct occasions. This includes twenty-one explicit presentations as the angel of the Lord, two as the angel of God, two as *his angel,* and one as a mighty angel. It remains now to analyze the nature of the angel of the Lord and to finally determine his identity.

CHAPTER FOUR

THE NATURE OF THE ANGEL OF THE LORD

The designation of an angel as the angel of the Lord is the most recurrent connotation of an angel found in Scripture. And not only that, but there is a vast and manifold difference between angels in general and the angel of the Lord in particular. So much so that it is imperative to carefully and critically examine the very nature of the angel of the Lord. Although including his basic constitution and disposition, his inherent qualities and distinction, it is his very being and substance—his essence—that we are searching. Just as was expressed for the angels of God, and perhaps more so, our evidence, research, inferences and deductions are restricted to the Bible, specifically those references to the angel of the Lord, whether by name or allusion. Not that this limits us in any way, much to the contrary, it is the only rational, logical, and sound conclusion.

The appearance of the angel of the Lord

Although the angel of the Lord was seen on a number of occasions (Exo 3:2; Judg 6:12; 1 Chr 21:16), and even recognized by animals (Num 22:23,25,27), he is only described physically four times. All the portraits, however, are of one consensus:

And Jacob was left alone; and there wrestled a man with him until the breaking of the day. -- Gen 32:24

And it came to pass, when Joshua was by

Jericho, that he lifted up his eyes and looked,
and, behold, there stood a man over against
him with his sword drawn in his hand: and
Joshua went unto him, and said unto him, Art
thou for us, or for our adversaries? -- Josh 5:13

Then the woman came and told her husband,
saying, A man of God came unto me, and his
countenance was like the countenance of an
angel of God, very terrible: but I asked him not
whence he was, neither told he me his name: --
Judg 13:6

I saw by night, and behold a man riding upon a
red horse, and he stood among the myrtle trees
that were in the bottom; and behind him were
there red horses, speckled, and white. -- Zec 1:8

This recognition of the angel of the Lord as a man is
commensurate to angels in general, hence it is under-
standable that he is often described in diverse ways as
just an angel:

The Angel which redeemed me from all evil,
bless the lads; and let my name be named on
them, and the name of my fathers Abraham
and Isaac; and let them grow into a multitude
in the midst of the earth. -- Gen 48:16

Behold, I send an Angel before thee, to keep
thee in the way, and to bring thee into the
place which I have prepared. -- Exo 23:20

And the angel of God, which went before the
camp of Israel, removed and went behind
them; and the pillar of the cloud went from
before their face, and stood behind them: -- Exo
14:19

My God hath sent his angel, and hath shut the
lions' mouths, that they have not hurt me:
forasmuch as before him innocency was found
in me; and also before thee, O king, have I done
no hurt. -- Dan 6:22

The demeanor of the angel of the Lord

The demeanor of the angel of the Lord depended on

the purpose for which he intervened in the affairs of men. He appeared as an adversary to Balaam (Num 22:22), an encourager to Gideon (Judg 6:12-14), a wrestler to Jacob (Gen 32:24), an officer to Joshua (Josh 5:13-14), and a cook (1 Kings 19:6) and an informant (2 Kings 1:3) to Elijah. He was a prophet to Hagar (Gen 16:10-12), Manoah's wife (Judg 13:3-5), and Matthew (Mat 1:20-21). He was a leader (Exo 14:19) and commander (Exo 23:20-23) to the children of Israel, but was also their rebuker (Judg 2:1-4). He was a destroyer to the inhabitants of Jerusalem (1 Chr 21:15), an assassin to the Assyrians (2 Kings 19:35), and an executioner to Herod (Acts 12:23). The angel of the Lord was an antagonist to David's persecutors (Ps 35:5-6) and a deliverer to them that fear God (Ps 34:7). Three times we are told the angel of the Lord had a sword in his hand (Num 22:23; Josh 5:13; 1 Chr 21:16). No wonder men were afraid of him (1 Chr 21:30; Mat 28:3; Luke 2:9)! In fact, Gideon thought that he would die because he saw him (Judg 6:22-23).

The abilities of the angel of the Lord

The ability of the angel of the Lord to perform various tasks can be classified under two categories: natural and mental. By natural we mean physical, visceral, and material. Three times we read that the angel of the Lord called someone **"out of heaven"** (Gen 21:17, 22:11, 22:15). Whatever the exact distance from earth to heaven, no audio device known to man of any frequency could span such a distance. David disclosed that he **"saw the angel of the Lord stand between the earth and the heaven"** (1 Chr 21:16). Considering the aforementioned distance between earth and heaven, for David to see him so juxtaposed means that the angel of the Lord would have to have assumed tremendous proportions. This coincides with his ability to appear and disappear at will. The record states that the angel of the Lord appeared to Moses (Exo 3:2), Gideon (Judg 6:12),

Manoah's wife (Judg 13:3), and both Manoah and his wife (Judg 13:21). But he also appeared (sans the term) physically, evidently out of nowhere, to Balaam (Num 22:21) and his ass (Num 22:25), Elijah (1 Kg 19:7), David (1 Chr 21:16), Joshua (Judg 5:13), Zechariah (Zec 1:11), Daniel (Dan 6:22), Nebuchadnezzar (Dan 3:28), shepherds (Luke 2:9), Philip (Acts 8:26), the apostles collectively (Acts 5:19), Peter (Acts 12:7) and Paul (Acts 27:23) individually, and apparently, to Hagar (Gen 16:7). This naturally implies that he could disappear:

> **Then the angel of the LORD put forth the end of the staff that was in his hand, and touched the flesh and the unleavened cakes; and there rose up fire out of the rock, and consumed the flesh and the unleavened cakes. Then the angel of the LORD departed out of his sight. -- Judg 6:21**

> **For it came to pass, when the flame went up toward heaven from off the altar, that the angel of the LORD ascended in the flame of the altar. And Manoah and his wife looked on it, and fell on their faces to the ground. -- Judg 13:20**

> **When they were past the first and the second ward, they came unto the iron gate that leadeth unto the city; which opened to them of his own accord: and they went out, and passed on through one street; and forthwith the angel departed from him. -- Acts 12:10**

This brings up one element that is connected with the angel of the Lord, whether appearing, disappearing, or remaining present: fire. He appeared to Moses **"in a flame of fire out of the midst of a bush"** (Exo 3:2), he left Manoah and his wife **"in the flame of the altar"** (Judg 13:20), he produced fire **"out of the rock"** (Judg 6:21) to consume the offering of Gideon, and dwelt in **"a pillar of fire"** (Exo 13:21). The angel of the Lord was also one of the last things some people saw before their untimely demise:

> **And it came to pass that night, that the angel of**

the LORD went out, and smote in the camp of
the Assyrians an hundred fourscore and five
thousand: and when they arose early in the
morning, behold, they were all dead corpses. --
2 Ki 19:35

And God sent an angel unto Jerusalem to
destroy it: and as he was destroying, the LORD
beheld, and he repented him of the evil, and
said to the angel that destroyed, It is enough,
stay now thine hand. And the angel of the
LORD stood by the threshingfloor of Ornan the
Jebusite. -- 1 Chr 21:15

And immediately the angel of the Lord smote
him, because he gave not God the glory: and he
was eaten of worms, and gave up the ghost. --
Acts 12:23

The supernatural power of the angel of the Lord is
evident. Certainly the angel of the Lord had no trouble
when he **"shut the lion's mouths"** (Dan 6:22) and
rolled back a great stone (Mat 28:2). Twice he broke
God's men out of prison:

But the angel of the Lord by night opened the
prison doors, and brought them forth, and said,
-- Acts 5:19

And, behold, the angel of the Lord came upon
him, and a light shined in the prison: and he
smote Peter on the side, and raised him up,
saying, Arise up quickly. And his chains fell off
from his hands. -- Acts 12:7

We are also told that the angel of the Lord brought the
children of Israel into their land (Exo 23:20, Judg 2:1),
no small feat considering that the men alone numbered
600,000 (Exo 12:37).

The mental and spiritual abilities of the angel of the
Lord are just as significant. The angel of the Lord found
one woman, Hagar (Gen 16:7), who was wandering in
the wilderness at the time. He straightway informed her
that she would **"bear a son"** (Gen 16:11). He told the
same thing to Manoah's wife (Judg 13:3), another barren
woman. The angel of the Lord smote Herod **"im-**

mediately" (Acts 12:23) after Herod **"gave not God the glory"** (Acts 12:23). He appeared to men in dreams (Gen 31:11; Mat 1:20, 2:13) and was aware of how much Elijah should eat (1 Kings 19:7). He ascertained the schemes of kings (2 Kings 1:2-3) and knew just where to send a preacher (Acts 8:26).

The relationship of the angel of the Lord

The fact that the angel of the Lord is so termed likewise bears mention. This indicates that he was faithful to, and represented, God himself. In addition to this designation, it should be remembered that he was also called **"the angel of God"** (Gen 21:17, 31:11; Ex 14:19; Judg 6:20, 13:9; Acts 27:23), **"his angel"** (Gen 24:7, 24:40; Dan 3:28, 6:22; Acts 12:4), **"the angel of his presence"** (Isa 63:9), and referred to by God as **"mine angel"** (Exo 23:23, 32:34). God's name was even said to be **"in him"** (Exo 23:21). Thus it is clear that the angel of the Lord bears a special relationship to God.

The work of the angel of the Lord

Considering the relationship of the angel of the Lord, it comes as no surprise that he acted at God's behest and sought to bring glory to him. He mentions God when he appears to Hagar (Gen 16:11), to Gideon (Judg 6:12), and to Manoah's wife (Judg 13:5); likewise when he calls to Abraham (Gen 22:12) and to Hagar later (Gen 21:17). He also appeared to Moses concerning the affliction of God's people (Exo 3:7). At the Lord's command he smote the Assyrians (2 Kings 19:35) and would have destroyed Jerusalem (1 Chr 21:15). The angel of the Lord purposed to honor and glorify God. He instructed Manoah: **"If thou wilt offer a burnt offering, thou must offer it unto the Lord"** (Judg 13:16) and commanded that David should **"set up an altar unto the Lord"** (1 Chr 21:18). He smote Herod because he **"gave not God the glory"** (Acts 12:23) and came to Elijah regarding Ahaziah's idolatry (2 Kings 1:3).

The deity of the angel of the Lord

There is one aspect to the nature of the angel of the Lord that underlies and sustains all others. The angel of the Lord did not always make an appearance to the subjects of his intervention. His demeanor was diverse and contingent, his abilities vast and eclectic. His relationship and work, although portentous and significant, is not climatic and determinative. The essence of his nature, the quintessence of his being, is that it is divine. The angel of the Lord did not merely have a relationship with God or simply do God's bidding, he did not just bring glory to God: he was God. The deity of the angel of the Lord is supported by Scripture in three ways: inference, comparison, declaration.

The first instance in which the deity of the angel of the Lord is apparent is the first mention of him in the Bible and is substantiated both by inference and declaration. The event was Hagar fleeing from Sarah:

> **And the angel of the LORD found her by a fountain of water in the wilderness, by the fountain in the way to Shur. And he said, Hagar, Sarai's maid, whence camest thou? and whither wilt thou go? And she said, I flee from the face of my mistress Sarai. And the angel of the LORD said unto her, Return to thy mistress, and submit thyself under her hands. And the angel of the LORD said unto her, I will multiply thy seed exceedingly, that it shall not be numbered for multitude. And the angel of the LORD said unto her, Behold, thou art with child, and shalt bear a son, and shalt call his name Ishmael; because the LORD hath heard thy affliction. And he will be a wild man; his hand will be against every man, and every man's hand against him; and he shall dwell in the presence of all his brethren. And she called the name of the LORD that spake unto her, Thou God seest me: for she said, Have I also here looked after him that seeth me? Wherefore the well was called Beerlahairoi; behold, it is between Kadesh and Bered. -- Gen 16:7-14**

There are two allusions here to the deity of the angel of the Lord, one brief, and the other quite involved, plus a succinct direct indication. Although it was the angel of the Lord who found and spoke to Hagar, as well as gave her the name of her son, the reason given was **"because the Lord hath heard thy affliction"** (Gen 16:11). On the other hand, it could be argued that because the Lord heard her affliction, he sent an ordinary angel to help her. But such was not the case here, for Hagar ascribes deity to the angel of the Lord, calling him **"the Lord"** and **"God"** (Gen 16:13).

The other inference to the deity of the angel of the Lord pertains to his statement to Hagar: **"I will multiply thy seed exceedingly, that it shall not be numbered for multitude"** (Gen 16:10). There are three ways that this assertion exhibits the deity of the angel of the Lord. This statement regarding the multiplication of seed was later given by the angel of the Lord to Abraham (Gen 22:17), the context of which clearly shows that the angel of the Lord was God himself. The second manner in which the deity of the angel of the Lord is implied is similar to the first, but this time God himself does do the speaking:

> **And I will make thy seed as the dust of the earth: so that if a man can number the dust of the earth, then shall thy seed also be numbered. -- Gen 13:16**

This is given again under the simile of stars in Genesis 15:5 and later repeated to Isaac (Gen 26:4,24), his wife (Gen 24:60), and Jacob (Gen 28:14, 32:12, 48:4). The third concerns God making the same statement but relating to Ishmael:

> **And also of the son of the bondwoman will I make a nation, because he is thy seed. -- Gen 21:13**

So like God, the angel of the Lord is responsible for the expansive multiplication of a seed, making it a great nation. It should also be noticed that the promise of a seed acquiring their own land was only made to the descendants of Abraham through Isaac (Gen 26:3, 28:13; Exo 33:1; Deu 34:4).

The next account of a suggestion of the deity of the angel of the Lord also concerns Hagar in the wilderness, this time with Ishmael:

> **And she went, and sat her down over against him a good way off, as it were a bowshot: for she said, Let me not see the death of the child. And she sat over against him, and lift up her voice, and wept. And God heard the voice of the lad; and the angel of God called to Hagar out of heaven, and said unto her, What aileth thee, Hagar? fear not; for God hath heard the voice of the lad where he is. Arise, lift up the lad, and hold him in thine hand; for I will make him a great nation. And God opened her eyes, and she saw a well of water; and she went, and filled the bottle with water, and gave the lad drink. -- Gen 21:16-19**

Once again we have the same two inferences. God hears and the angel of the Lord speaks (Gen 21:17) just like Genesis 16:11. And likewise, the angel of the Lord speaks, but God opens Hagar's eyes (Gen 21:18-19). What also holds true about the increase of Ishmael's posterity (Gen 16:10) applies here as well.

The third portrait of the angel of the Lord that reveals his deity is the narrative of Abraham and his frustrated sacrifice of Isaac. As Abraham **"took the knife to slay his son"** (Gen 22:10) he was averted by the angel of the Lord:

> **And the angel of the LORD called unto him out of heaven, and said, Abraham, Abraham: and he said, Here am I. And he said, Lay not thine hand upon the lad, neither do thou any thing unto him: for now I know that thou fearest God, seeing thou hast not withheld thy son, thine only son from me. And Abraham lifted up his eyes, and looked, and behold behind him a ram caught in a thicket by his horns: and Abraham went and took the ram, and offered**

him up for a burnt offering in the stead of his son. And Abraham called the name of that place Jehovahjireh: as it is said to this day, In the mount of the LORD it shall be seen. And the angel of the LORD called unto Abraham out of heaven the second time, And said, By myself have I sworn, saith the LORD, for because thou hast done this thing, and hast not withheld thy son, thine only son: That in blessing I will bless thee, and in multiplying I will multiply thy seed as the stars of the heaven, and as the sand which is upon the sea shore; and thy seed shall possess the gate of his enemies; And in thy seed shall all the nations of the earth be blessed; because thou hast obeyed my voice. -- Gen 22:11-18

This account contains three references to the deity of the angel of the Lord: one by inference, one by comparison, and one by direct affirmation. The first is an allusion to the deity of the angel of the Lord much like we have encountered earlier. The angel of the Lord, in calling Abraham from heaven, tells him: **"For now I know that thou fearest God"** (Gen 22:12). By a comparison within the context of this account we can also ascertain direct proof for the deity of the angel of the Lord. The statement was made to Abraham by the angel of the Lord that **"thou hast not withheld thy son, thine only son from me"** (Gen 22:12). Yet it was God himself who commanded Abraham to offer his son (Gen 22:2), commended him for not withholding his son (Gen 22:16), and extolled him for obeying his voice (Gen 22:18). But the most prominent testimony for the deity of the angel of the Lord appears at the second calling of Abraham by the angel of the Lord (Gen 22:15). Here it is not Hagar (Gen 16:13), but the angel of the Lord who declares **"by myself have I sworn, saith the Lord"** (Gen 22:16), affirming his deity. The next account of the angel of the Lord contains a clear and concise declaration of the deity of the angel of the Lord. The character attended to by the angel of the Lord is Jacob; the occasion is his departure from Laban:

> **And the angel of God spake unto me in a dream, saying, Jacob: And I said, Here am I. And he said, Lift up now thine eyes, and see, all the rams which leap upon the cattle are ringstreaked, speckled, and grisled: for I have seen all that Laban doeth unto thee. I am the God of Bethel, where thou anointedst the pillar, and where thou vowedst a vow unto me: now arise, get thee out from this land, and return unto the land of thy kindred. -- Gen 31:11-13**

The angel of the Lord (here called the angel of God) claims to Jacob that he is the God of Bethel, the same God who earlier declared: **"I am the Lord God of Abraham thy father, and the God of Isaac"** (Gen 28:13).

There is yet another record of the angel of the Lord frequenting Jacob. This time he not only appears to him but wrestles with him as well:

> **And Jacob was left alone; and there wrestled a man with him until the breaking of the day. And when he saw that he prevailed not against him, he touched the hollow of his thigh; and the hollow of Jacob's thigh was out of joint, as he wrestled with him. And he said, Let me go, for the day breaketh. And he said, I will not let thee go, except thou bless me. And he said unto him, What is thy name? And he said, Jacob. And he said, Thy name shall be called no more Jacob, but Israel: for as a prince hast thou power with God and with men, and hast prevailed. And Jacob asked him, and said, Tell me, I pray thee, thy name. And he said, Wherefore is it that thou dost ask after my name? And he blessed him there. And Jacob called the name of the place Peniel: for I have seen God face to face, and my life is preserved. -- Gen 32:24-30**

That this was no ordinary man we have seen, for in Hosea 12:4 he is called **"the angel."** There are two references in this passage that explicitly prove the deity angel of the Lord, one from the mouth of the angel and

one from the mouth of Jacob. When the angel of the
Lord changed Jacob's name to Israel after wrestling with
him, the purpose stated by the angel was because Jacob
had **"power with God"** (Gen 32:28). Jacob certainly
believed this for he subsequently claimed to **"have seen
God face to face"** (Gen 32:30).

Reference is later made to this event where even
stronger proof for the deity of the angel of the Lord is
offered:

> **He took his brother by the heel in the womb,
> and by his strength he had power with God:
> Yea, he had power over the angel, and pre-
> vailed: he wept, and made supplication unto
> him: he found him in Bethel, and there he
> spake with us; Even the LORD God of hosts;
> the LORD is his memorial. -- Hosea 12:3-5**

Two direct asseverations for the deity of the angel of the
Lord are here presented. Jacob wrestled with **"a man"**
(Gen 32:24) who was said to be **"the angel"** (Hosea
12:4), yet he **"had power with God"** (Hosea 12:4). The
second example can be seen in the words of God in which
he equates **"the angel"** (Hosea 12:4) with **"the Lord
God of hosts"** (Hosea 12:5).

The final occurrence in Genesis of some evidence for
the deity of the angel of the Lord is in a mention of him
by Jacob in which he positively identifies him as God:

> **And he blessed Joseph, and said, God, before
> whom my fathers Abraham and Isaac did walk,
> the God which fed me all my life long unto this
> day, The Angel which redeemed me from all
> evil, bless the lads; and let my name be named
> on them, and the name of my fathers Abraham
> and Isaac; and let them grow into a multitude
> in the midst of the earth. -- Gen 48:16**

It is evident that **"the angel"** (Gen 48:16) is here
substituted for **"God"** (Gen 48:15).

The next mention of the angel of the Lord where we
find evidence for his deity is the account of Moses at the
burning bush. This story is replete with references to the

deity of the angel of the Lord, with two inferences to, and three definite assertions of his deity:

> **And the angel of the LORD appeared unto him in a flame of fire out of the midst of a bush: and he looked, and, behold, the bush burned with fire, and the bush was not consumed. And Moses said, I will now turn aside, and see this great sight, why the bush is not burnt. And when the LORD saw that he turned aside to see, God called unto him out of the midst of the bush, and said, Moses, Moses. And he said, Here am I. And he said, Draw not nigh hither: put off thy shoes from off thy feet, for the place whereon thou standest is holy ground. Moreover he said, I am the God of thy father, the God of Abraham, the God of Isaac, and the God of Jacob. And Moses hid his face; for he was afraid to look upon God. -- Exo 3:2-6**

To begin with, this angel appears in a **"flame of fire"** (Exo 3:2) without burning up. And secondly, his presence causes the soil to be **"holy ground"** (Exo 3:5). As if this were not enough, three times the angel of the Lord is indisputable said to be God. Although the angel of the Lord was in the burning bush, **"God called unto him out of the midst of the bush"** (Exo 3:4). He then vocalized that he was **"the God of thy father, the God of Abraham, the God of Isaac, and the God of Jacob"** (Exo 3:6). Moses undoubtedly recognized this for he **"hid his face; for he was afraid to look upon God"** (Exo 3:6). The deity here of the angel of the Lord is further confirmed by the ensuing dialogue between God and Moses in which the narrative further relates what **"the Lord said"** (Exo 3:7) or **"God said"** (Exo 3:14,15), as well as Moses' reply **"unto God"** (Exo 3:11,13). Stephen's account of this event in the New Testament provides additional support for the deity of the angel of the Lord (Acts 7:30-34). The only difference being that he refers to the angel as **"an angel of the Lord"** (Acts 7:30).

Once the children of Israel made it out of Egypt, the

angel of the Lord led them through the Red Sea. This
furnishes us with still another account of his deity:

> **And the angel of God, which went before the
> camp of Israel, removed and went behind
> them; and the pillar of the cloud went from
> before their face, and stood behind them: And
> it came between the camp of the Egyptians and
> the camp of Israel; and it was a cloud and
> darkness to them, but it gave light by night to
> these: so that the one came not near the other
> all the night. -- Exo 14:19-20**

There are two confirmations of the deity of the angel of
the Lord by comparing this with two statements
touching the cloud:

> **And the LORD went before them by day in a
> pillar of a cloud, to lead them the way; and by
> night in a pillar of fire, to give them light; to go
> by day and night: -- Exo 13:21**

> **And it came to pass, that in the morning watch
> the LORD looked unto the host of the Egyp-
> tians through the pillar of fire and of the cloud,
> and troubled the host of the Egyptians, -- Exo
> 14:24**

Like God, the angel of God **"went before"** (Exo 13:21,
14:19) the children of Israel. That he also dwelt in the
cloud can be seen by observing that when the cloud
moved, he moved. Thus the fact that God had to look
through the cloud is further evidence for the deity of the
angel of the Lord.

The other mention of the angel of the Lord in Exodus
includes two implications of his deity in addition to a
proof by comparison and a candid declaration. This is not
an actual appearance but rather a statement made by
God:

> **Behold, I send an Angel before thee, to keep
> thee in the way, and to bring thee into the
> place which I have prepared. Beware of him,
> and obey his voice, provoke him not; for he will
> not pardon your transgressions: for my name is
> in him. But if thou shalt indeed obey his voice,**

> **and do all that I speak; then I will be an enemy
> unto thine enemies, and an adversary unto
> thine adversaries. For mine Angel shall go
> before thee, and bring thee in unto the Amor-
> ites, and the Hittites, and the Perizzites, and
> the Canaanites, the Hivites, and the Jebusites:
> and I will cut them off. -- Exo 23:20-23**

The angel of the Lord, it is here acknowledged, has the
authority to pardon transgressions. This is reminiscent
of God himself:

> **I acknowledged my sin unto thee, and mine
> iniquity have I not hid. I said, I will confess my
> transgressions unto the LORD; and thou for-
> gavest the iniquity of my sin. Selah. -- Psa 32:5**

> **And the scribes and the Pharisees began to
> reason, saying, Who is this which speaketh
> blasphemies? Who can forgive sins, but God
> alone? -- Luke 5:21**

That this was no ordinary angel is also apparent from
the fact that God's **"name is in him"** (Exo 23:21).

By comparison of Scripture with Scripture we can
also see another testimony for the deity of the angel of
the Lord. God's angel, it is said, will bring the children
of Israel **"in unto the Amorites, and the Hittites,
and the Perizzites, and the Canaanites, and the
Hivites, and the Jebusites"** (Exo 23:23). But we were
previously told that God would bring them in:

> **And I have said, I will bring you up out of the
> affliction of Egypt unto the land of the Canaan-
> ites, and the Hittites, and the Amorites, and the
> Perizzites, and the Hivites, and the Jebusites,
> unto a land flowing with milk and honey. -- Exo
> 3:17**

> **And it shall be when the LORD shall bring thee
> into the land of the Canaanites, and the
> Hittites, and the Amorites, and the Hivites, and
> the Jebusites, which he sware unto thy fathers
> to give thee, a land flowing with milk and
> honey, that thou shalt keep this service in this
> month. -- Exo 13:5**

A clear picture of the deity of the angel of the Lord is in view in the remark: **"But if thou shalt indeed obey his voice, and do all that I speak"** (Exo 23:22). Obeying the voice of the angel of the Lord is the same as doing what God spoke.

The lone account of the angel of the Lord in Numbers furnishes us with three suggestions of the deity of the angel of the Lord and one proof by comparison. The men involved are Balaam and his two servants, along with an ass, although there is no record that the two servants actually saw the angel of the Lord. The inferences to the deity of the angel of the Lord once again involve God and the angel working together:

> **And God's anger was kindled because he went: and the angel of the LORD stood in the way for an adversary against him. Now he was riding upon his ass, and his two servants were with him. -- Num 22:22**

> **And when the ass saw the angel of the LORD, she fell down under Balaam: and Balaam's anger was kindled, and he smote the ass with a staff. And the LORD opened the mouth of the ass, and she said unto Balaam, What have I done unto thee, that thou hast smitten me these three times? -- Num 22:27-28**

> **Then the LORD opened the eyes of Balaam, and he saw the angel of the LORD standing in the way, and his sword drawn in his hand: and he bowed down his head, and fell flat on his face. -- Num 22:31**

God speaks and the angel of the Lord immediately acts, as though they were one and the same.

The other proof for the deity of the angel of the Lord is found by comparing a statement made by the angel of the Lord with a comparable assertion by God:

> **And the angel of the LORD said unto Balaam, Go with the men: but only the word that I shall speak unto thee, that thou shalt speak. So Balaam went with the princes of Balak. -- Num 22:35**

And God came unto Balaam at night, and said unto him, If the men come to call thee, rise up, and go with them; but yet the word which I shall say unto thee, that shalt thou do. -- Num 22:20

This concludes the proofs for the deity of the angel of the Lord in the Pentateuch. Out of eight manifestations of the angel of the Lord, a reference to one of them, and two other mentions of him, we have already seen evidence for his deity by eleven inferences, five comparisons with other Scriptures, and twelve direct declarations.

The angel of the Lord in Joshua appears under another title and gives us confirmation of his deity both by inference and by correlation with an earlier passage:

And it came to pass, when Joshua was by Jericho, that he lifted up his eyes and looked, and, behold, there stood a man over against him with his sword drawn in his hand: and Joshua went unto him, and said unto him, Art thou for us, or for our adversaries? And he said, Nay; but as captain of the host of the LORD am I now come. And Joshua fell on his face to the earth, and did worship, and said unto him, What saith my lord unto his servant? And the captain of the LORD'S host said unto Joshua, Loose thy shoe from off thy foot; for the place whereon thou standest is holy. And Joshua did so. -- Josh 5:13-15

Here the angel of the Lord announces to Joshua that because of his presence the ground is holy. This is a strong allusion to his deity. Yet by comparison of his statement with what was recorded earlier concerning the angel of the Lord at the burning bush, we can see even greater indication of the deity of the angel of the Lord:

And he said, Draw not nigh hither: put off thy shoes from off thy feet, for the place whereon thou standest is holy ground. -- Exo 3:5

Since the angel of the Lord was explicitly declared to be God himself appearing in the burning bush, it therefore follows that such is the case here in Joshua. Another suggestion of the deity of the angel of the Lord is the fact that he accepted worship that is reserved for God alone:

> **For thou shalt worship no other god: for the LORD, whose name is Jealous, is a jealous God: -- Exo 34:14**

> **Then saith Jesus unto him, Get thee hence, Satan: for it is written, Thou shalt worship the Lord thy God, and him only shalt thou serve. -- Mat 4:10**

The book of Judges furnishes us with three appearances of the angel of the Lord, and all three provide further evidence for the deity of the angel of the Lord. The first is his appearance to the children of Israel:

> **And an angel of the LORD came up from Gilgal to Bochim, and said, I made you to go up out of Egypt, and have brought you unto the land which I sware unto your fathers; and I said, I will never break my covenant with you. And ye shall make no league with the inhabitants of this land; ye shall throw down their altars: but ye have not obeyed my voice: why have ye done this? Wherefore I also said, I will not drive them out from before you; but they shall be as thorns in your sides, and their gods shall be a snare unto you. And it came to pass, when the angel of the LORD spake these words unto all the children of Israel, that the people lifted up their voice, and wept. -- Judg 2:1-4**

There are five phrases here spoken by the angel of the Lord that, when compared with other Scriptures, yield still more proof for the deity of the angel of the Lord. The first is his claim: **"I made you to go up out of Egypt"** (Judg 2:1). There are only four examples in Scripture of someone said to bring Israel out of Egypt. Although one time we read that the children of Israel **"went forth out of the land of Egypt with their armies under the hand of Moses and Aaron"** (Num 33:1), and a few others times just **"Moses, the man that brought us out of the land of Egypt"** (Ex 32:1), plus Israel once saying concerning the molten calf: **"These be thy gods, O Israel, which brought thee up out of the land of Egypt"** (Exo 32:4), the overwhelming majority of the time we are told that the Lord God brought them out. This was predicated both before, the very day, and after the actual event:

> **And ye shall observe the feast of unleavened bread; for in this selfsame day have I brought your armies out of the land of Egypt: therefore shall ye observe this day in your generations by an ordinance for ever. -- Exo 12:17**

> **And it came to pass the selfsame day, that the LORD did bring the children of Israel out of the land of Egypt by their armies. -- Exo 12:51**

> **I am the LORD thy God, which have brought thee out of the land of Egypt, out of the house of bondage. -- Exo 20:2**

So the inescapable conclusion is that the angel of the Lord brought the children of Israel up out of Egypt: because he was God.

The other four statements are just as conclusive. The angel of the Lord said that he brought Israel **"unto the land which I sware unto your fathers"** (Judg 2:1) and so did God:

> **All the commandments which I command thee this day shall ye observe to do, that ye may live, and multiply, and go in and possess the land which the LORD sware unto your fathers. -- Deu 8:1**

The angel of the Lord professed to have said: **"I will never break my covenant with you"** (Judg 2:1), but God said it:

> **And yet for all that, when they be in the land of their enemies, I will not cast them away, neither will I abhor them, to destroy them utterly, and to break my covenant with them: for I am the LORD their God. -- Lev 26:44**

The angel of the Lord maintained that the children of

Israel disobeyed him because they didn't **"throw down"** (Judg 2:2) the altars of the heathen, yet God was the one who made the command:

> **Take heed to thyself, lest thou make a covenant with the inhabitants of the land whither thou goest, lest it be for a snare in the midst of thee: But ye shall destroy their altars, break their images, and cut down their groves: -- Exo 34:12-13**

The angel of the Lord also related the penalty for their disobedience: **"They shall be as thorns in your sides"** (Judg 2:3), but it was the Lord God who was the original author:

> **But if ye will not drive out the inhabitants of the land from before you; then it shall come to pass, that those which ye let remain of them shall be pricks in your eyes, and thorns in your sides, and shall vex you in the land wherein ye dwell. -- Num 33:55**

The next account in Judges concerns the appearance of the angel of the Lord to Gideon. Two events take place, the first of which presents us with a firm declaration of the deity of the angel of the Lord:

> **And there came an angel of the LORD, and sat under an oak which was in Ophrah, that pertained unto Joash the Abiezrite: and his son Gideon threshed wheat by the winepress, to hide it from the Midianites. And the angel of the LORD appeared unto him, and said unto him, The LORD is with thee, thou mighty man of valour. And Gideon said unto him, Oh my Lord, if the LORD be with us, why then is all this befallen us? and where be all his miracles which our fathers told us of, saying, Did not the LORD bring us up from Egypt? but now the LORD hath forsaken us, and delivered us into the hands of the Midianites. And the LORD looked upon him, and said, Go in this thy might, and thou shalt save Israel from the hand of the Midianites: have not I sent thee? And he said unto him, Oh my Lord, wherewith**

> shall I save Israel? behold, my family is poor in
> Manasseh, and I am the least in my father's
> house. And the LORD said unto him, Surely I
> will be with thee, and thou shalt smite the
> Midianites as one man. -- Judg 6:11-16

Although the angel of the Lord is standing in front of
Gideon, it is declared that **"the Lord looked upon
him"** (Judg 6:14).

The second encounter Gideon has with the angel of
the Lord implies his deity due to the unusual event that
takes place:

> Then the angel of the LORD put forth the end
> of the staff that was in his hand, and touched
> the flesh and the unleavened cakes; and there
> rose up fire out of the rock, and consumed the
> flesh and the unleavened cakes. Then the angel
> of the LORD departed out of his sight. -- Judg
> 6:21

A sacrifice meets a similar end during the days of Elijah:

> Then the fire of the LORD fell, and consumed
> the burnt sacrifice, and the wood, and the
> stones, and the dust, and licked up the water
> that was in the trench. -- 1 Ki 18:38

The final narrative of the angel of the Lord in Judges
contains an allusion to the deity of the angel of the Lord
as well as a direct affirmation:

> And Manoah said unto the angel of the LORD, I
> pray thee, let us detain thee, until we shall
> have made ready a kid for thee. And the angel
> of the LORD said unto Manoah, Though thou
> detain me, I will not eat of thy bread: and if
> thou wilt offer a burnt offering, thou must offer
> it unto the LORD. For Manoah knew not that
> he was an angel of the LORD. And Manoah said
> unto the angel of the LORD, What is thy name,
> that when thy sayings come to pass we may do
> thee honour? And the angel of the LORD said
> unto him, Why askest thou thus after my name,
> seeing it is secret? So Manoah took a kid with a
> meat offering, and offered it upon a rock unto
> the LORD: and the angel did wonderously; and

> **Manoah and his wife looked on. For it came to pass, when the flame went up toward heaven from off the altar, that the angel of the LORD ascended in the flame of the altar. And Manoah and his wife looked on it, and fell on their faces to the ground. But the angel of the LORD did no more appear to Manoah and to his wife. Then Manoah knew that he was an angel of the LORD. And Manoah said unto his wife, We shall surely die, because we have seen God. -- Judg 13:15-22**

A strong indication of the deity of the angel of the Lord can be seen in how he makes his exit. Like his appearance in the burning bush, the fire has no effect on him. The frank avowal of the angel's deity is apparent by the reaction of Manoah: **"We shall surely die, because we have seen God"** (Judg 13:22).

A mention of the angel of the Lord in Isaiah contributes another proof for his deity by way of a comparison with another passage of Scripture:

> **In all their affliction he was afflicted, and the angel of his presence saved them: in his love and in his pity he redeemed them; and he bare them, and carried them all the days of old. -- Isa 63:9**

> **And Moses said unto the LORD, See, thou sayest unto me, Bring up this people: and thou hast not let me know whom thou wilt send with me. Yet thou hast said, I know thee by name, and thou hast also found grace in my sight. Now therefore, I pray thee, if I have found grace in thy sight, show me now thy way, that I may know thee, that I may find grace in thy sight: and consider that this nation is thy people. And he said, My presence shall go with thee, and I will give thee rest. -- Exo 33:12-14**

The **"angel of his presence"** (Isa 63:9) that went with the children of Israel is here identified as God himself.

The book of Daniel contains one account of the angel of the Lord in which his deity is evident. Three Hebrews were cast into the **"burning fiery furnace"** (Dan 3:23) by Nebuchadnezzar, king of Babylon, yet he saw four men. A comparison of Nebuchadnezzar's remarks reveals the special character of the angel of the Lord:

> **He answered and said, Lo, I see four men loose, walking in the midst of the fire, and they have no hurt; and the form of the fourth is like the Son of God. -- Dan 3:25**

> **Then Nebuchadnezzar spake, and said, Blessed be the God of Shadrach, Meshach, and Abednego, who hath sent his angel, and delivered his servants that trusted in him, and have changed the king's word, and yielded their bodies, that they might not serve nor worship any god, except their own God. -- Dan 3:28**

The final references to the angel of the Lord in the Old Testament yield further evidence for his deity in the form of implication and affirmation. The scene is a vision of Zechariah:

> **And he showed me Joshua the high priest standing before the angel of the LORD, and Satan standing at his right hand to resist him. And the LORD said unto Satan, The LORD rebuke thee, O Satan; even the LORD that hath chosen Jerusalem rebuke thee: is not this a brand plucked out of the fire? Now Joshua was clothed with filthy garments, and stood before the angel. And he answered and spake unto those that stood before him, saying, Take away the filthy garments from him. And unto him he said, Behold, I have caused thine iniquity to pass from thee, and I will clothe thee with change of raiment. And I said, Let them set a fair mitre upon his head. So they set a fair mitre upon his head, and clothed him with garments. And the angel of the LORD stood by. And the angel of the LORD protested unto Joshua, saying, Thus saith the LORD of hosts; If thou wilt walk in my ways, and if thou wilt keep my charge, then thou shalt also judge my house, and shalt also keep my courts, and I will give thee places to walk among these that stand by. -- Zec 3:1-7**

When the angel of the Lord speaks, he is cited as **"the Lord"** (Zec 3:2). Although this is clear, the allusion to his deity, like we have seen elsewhere, could go either way. When the angel of the Lord speaks again, he begins with the formula: **"Thus saith the Lord"** (Zec 3:7). Often times this is obviously God speaking through a prophet:

> **In those days was Hezekiah sick unto death. And Isaiah the prophet the son of Amoz came unto him, and said unto him, Thus saith the LORD, Set thine house in order: for thou shalt die, and not live. -- Isa 38:1**

And sometimes it is God giving his instructions to a prophet:

> **Go, and say to Hezekiah, Thus saith the LORD, the God of David thy father, I have heard thy prayer, I have seen thy tears: behold, I will add unto thy days fifteen years. -- Isa 38:5**

But at other times, it is God himself speaking:

> **For thus saith the LORD that created the heavens; God himself that formed the earth and made it; he hath established it, he created it not in vain, he formed it to be inhabited: I am the LORD; and there is none else. -- Isa 45:18**

Therefore, the **"thus saith the Lord"** in Zechariah chapter three could be either God speaking through the angel of the Lord or God himself as the angel of the Lord speaking. So at the conclusion of the Old Testament, out of fourteen manifestations of the angel of the Lord, we have some forty-four references to the deity of the angel of the Lord, sixteen by inference, twelve by comparison, and sixteen by direct declaration.

Moving to the New Testament we find definite proof for the deity of the angel of the Lord in Stephen's account of Moses and the angel in the burning bush (Exo 7:30-34), but as this is a reference to what has already taken place in Exodus and adds no further information than that found there, we refer the reader back to the original account. The main occurrence of a proof for the deity of the angel of the Lord in the New Testament takes place during the shipwreck of Paul the Apostle and contains one direct declaration as well as two proofs by comparison with other Scriptures:

> **But after long abstinence Paul stood forth in the midst of them, and said, Sirs, ye should have hearkened unto me, and not have loosed from Crete, and to have gained this harm and loss. And now I exhort you to be of good cheer: for there shall be no loss of any man's life among you, but of the ship. For there stood by me this night the angel of God, whose I am, and whom I serve, Saying, Fear not, Paul; thou must be brought before Caesar: and, lo, God hath given thee all them that sail with thee. Wherefore, sirs, be of good cheer: for I believe God, that it shall be even as it was told me. -- Acts 27:21-25**

Paul maintained that he belonged to the angel of God and served him. Yet Paul was a servant of God:

> **Paul, a servant of Jesus Christ, called to be an apostle, separated unto the gospel of God, -- Rom 1:1**

> **I thank God, whom I serve from my forefathers with pure conscience, that without ceasing I have remembrance of thee in my prayers night and day; -- 2 Tim 1:3**

Paul served God because he, like all Christians, was his by purchase:

> **What? know ye not that your body is the temple of the Holy Ghost which is in you, which ye have of God, and ye are not your own? For ye are bought with a price: therefore glorify God in your body, and in your spirit, which are God's. -- 1 Cor 6:19-20**

And although the angel of God spoke to Paul (Acts 27:24), Paul implied that it was God who spoke to him (Acts 27:25).

The final testimonies for the deity of the angel of the

Lord are two inferences in Revelation. The angel of the Lord is here termed a **"mighty angel"** (Rev 10:1), but it is his countenance that is convincing:

> **And I saw another mighty angel come down from heaven, clothed with a cloud: and a rainbow was upon his head, and his face was as it were the sun, and his feet as pillars of fire: --**
> **Rev 10:1**

The description of this angel is like no other. But that is not all, for later he takes credit for the two witnesses who prophesy during the Tribulation:

> **And I will give power unto my two witnesses, and they shall prophesy a thousand two hundred and threescore days, clothed in sackcloth.**
> **-- Rev 11:3**

With the addition of these two cases in the New Testament, we now find that out of sixteen manifestations of the angel of the Lord, and four references to him, there are forty-nine instances where we find evidence for his deity: eighteen inferences, fourteen comparisons with other Scriptures, and seventeen explicit affirmations. But we are still faced with the question: who is the angel of the Lord?

CHAPTER FIVE

THE IDENTITY OF THE ANGEL OF THE LORD

The question was asked at the outset of this treatise: "Who is the angel of the Lord and what is his relationship to other angels and God himself?" That relationship we have seen is one of supremacy and preeminence to the angels in general and of coextensive deity as pertaining to God. The ascendancy of the angel of the Lord was never in question, but the well substantiated fact of his deity is a seemingly bitter pill to some "Christian" expositors who can not quite express the obvious conclusion:

> This seems to be identical with God.[1]

> Another possible interpretation is that God speaks so fully through the angel that he himself is virtually speaking.[2]

> The lack of precise data in the OT with regard to the identification of this figure and his relationship to Yahweh has given rise to a number of conclusions.[3]

> A messenger of God, almost equivalent to Deity, yet distinct from Him.[4]

This lack of precision is appalling since both secular and Jewish writers give credence to the established thesis as seen in comments concerning the appearance of the angel of the Lord in the burning bush:

> A strict interpretation of the use of the term would suggest that it is the Lord Himself who is the angel of the burning bush.[5]

> The angel of God calls to Moses from the burning bush (Ex 3:2), but the ensuing dialogue is conducted

with God himself.[6]

The problem is not due to any deficiency of applicable biblical evidence, for an abundance has been cited; no difficulty exists because of ambiguous language in the biblical narrative, for not only has the deity of the angel of the Lord been affirmed by inference and comparison but by direct declaration of the Scripture. The obstacle is unbelief.

Assuming that the angel of the Lord is who the Bible says he is, namely God, and basing this presumption on the clear sentiments of Scripture because it is here presupposed to be the authoritative the word of God, we are faced with a dilemma:

> **Who only hath immortality, dwelling in the light which no man can approach unto; whom no man hath seen, nor can see: to whom be honour and power everlasting. Amen. -- 1 Tim 6:16**

> **No man hath seen God at any time. If we love one another, God dwelleth in us, and his love is perfected in us. -- 1 John 4:12**

How can God, who is incorporeal, be seen? If the angel of the Lord was seen and yet was God, then we are faced with an apparent incompatibility in his identity. This brings up the very nature of God himself.

The nature of God

The nature of God is both the cause and the cure for our predicament. Although encompassing diverse elements, the **"divine nature"** (2 Pet 2:4), as evident to all except the adherents to Pantheism and Panentheism, is fundamentally spiritual:

> **God is a Spirit: and they that worship him must worship him in spirit and in truth. -- John 4:24**

God is said to have a spiritual essence that is both **"invisible"** (Col 1:15) and **"light"** (1 John 1:5). This appears to still further obscure the relationship between God and the angel of the Lord would it not be for the fact that orthodox Christianity is theistic, that there is a trinity of persons in the divine essence: one God in three persons. Although the designation trinity is not used in Scripture, another accurate term is, and coincidentally, it occurs three times:

> **Forasmuch then as we are the offspring of God, we ought not to think that the Godhead is like unto gold, or silver, or stone, graven by art and man's device. -- Acts 17:29**

> **For the invisible things of him from the creation of the world are clearly seen, being understood by the things that are made, even his eternal power and Godhead; so that they are without excuse: -- Rom 1:20**

> **For in him dwelleth all the fulness of the Godhead bodily. -- Col 2:9**

The trinity is the only plausible explanation of God since the Bible unequivocally maintains the twin truths of the singularity and unity of God:

> **Ye are my witnesses, saith the LORD, and my servant whom I have chosen: that ye may know and believe me, and understand that I am he: before me there was no God formed, neither shall there be after me. -- Isa 43:10**

> **Hear, O Israel: The LORD our God is one LORD: -- Deu 6:4**

That there is a plurality in the Godhead can most notably be seen in the plural expressions used by God when speaking of himself:

> **And God said, Let us make man in our image, after our likeness: and let them have dominion over the fish of the sea, and over the fowl of the air, and over the cattle, and over all the earth, and over every creeping thing that creepeth upon the earth. -- Gen 1:26**

> **Also I heard the voice of the Lord, saying, Whom shall I send, and who will go for us?**

Then said I, Here am I; send me. -- Isa 6:8

And that this plurality involves a trinity of persons in the Godhead can be verified by their actual identification in both Testaments:

> **Come ye near unto me, hear ye this; I have not spoken in secret from the beginning; from the time that it was, there am I: and now the Lord GOD, and his Spirit, hath sent me. -- Isa 48:16**

> **But when the Comforter is come, whom I will send unto you from the Father, even the Spirit of truth, which proceedeth from the Father, he shall testify of me: -- John 15:26**

It is not the trinity itself, however, but the real and personal distinction that exists among its persons that resolves our dilemma. Now that we know that God can be incorporeal and yet still be distinguished, we are left to determine the manner in which this is carried out.

The manifestation of God

It has been established with certainty that the angel of the Lord was in fact an appearance of God himself. These are called Theophanies by the theologians. It was also expressed that the apparent problem of how an incorporeal being could be manifest physically was both caused and cured by an element of the nature of God, namely, the differentiation among the persons of the Godhead. This is so crucial that the stated deity of the angel of the Lord demands the Trinity for its authenticity. Although not in any fashion denying the Trinity, the significance of the angel of the Lord is sometimes disparaged:

> We should not see the angel of the Lord as either a premature form of the incarnation or as an early revelation of the Trinity.[7]

> The angel is a later interpretation and the story was first told of Yahweh himself.[8]

> When ultimately, under the Mosaic dispensation, the holy character and the real nature of Jahweh began

to be apprehended, the belief that He personally appeared among men necessarily became more and more untenable; hence, while Jahweh Himself receded further from men, His messenger, or angel, appeared in His stead, and became His representative in all His dealings with men.[9]

The idea of the Christian trinity of the Father, Son, and Holy Spirit being presupposed, a brief look at each member of the Godhead in his mode of subsistence will show us the manner in which God manifests himself.

God the Father has the relative property of paternity, hence he is called **"the Father of our Lord Jesus Christ"** (2 Cor 1:3). His likeness is described by John:

> **And immediately I was in the spirit; and, behold, a throne was set in heaven, and one sat on the throne. And he that sat was to look upon like a jasper and a sardine stone: and there was a rainbow round about the throne, in sight like unto an emerald. -- Rev 4:2-3**

God the Holy Spirit, to whom belongs the personal relation of spiration, is denominated analogously **"wind"** (Ezek 37:6), **"breath"** (Ezek 37:9) and **"spirit"** (Ezek 37:14), and is the breath of God:

> **The spirit of God hath made me, and the breath of the Almighty hath given me life. -- Job 33:4**

> **By the word of the LORD were the heavens made; and all the host of them by the breath of his mouth. -- Psa 33:6**

This leaves us with **"the only begotten of the Father"** (John 1:14), of whom **"God giveth not the Spirit by measure unto him"** (John 3:34), the **"son of God"** (John 1:34): the Lord Jesus Christ. The Godhead is only manifested in **"the way"** (John 14:6) revealed in the Bible:

> **Jesus saith unto him, Have I been so long time with you, and yet hast thou not known me, Philip? he that hath seen me hath seen the Father; and how sayest thou then, Show us the**

Father? -- John 14:9

Who is the image of the invisible God, the firstborn of every creature: -- Col 1:15

For in him dwelleth all the fulness of the Godhead bodily. -- Col 2:9

And without controversy great is the mystery of godliness: God was manifest in the flesh, justified in the Spirit, seen of angels, preached unto the Gentiles, believed on in the world, received up into glory. -- 1 Tim 3:16

Therefore, if there is only one God, and the angel of the Lord is God, then Jesus Christ is the angel of the Lord because he is the appearance of God, the **"brightness of his glory, and the express image of his person"** (Heb 1:3).

This would also be the case where God appears in the Old Testament, but no mention is made of the angel of the Lord. A notable example would be God's appearance to Abraham before the destruction of Sodom and Gomorrah when he came with two others:

And the LORD appeared unto him in the plains of Mamre: and he sat in the tent door in the heat of the day; And he lift up his eyes and looked, and, lo, three men stood by him: and when he saw them, he ran to meet them from the tent door, and bowed himself toward the ground, -- Gen 18:1-2

These men are identified as the angels who God sent to destroy Sodom and Gomorrah (Gen 19:1,13). But notice another declaration of the deity of the angel of the Lord in the narrative of the destruction of the cities:

Then the LORD rained upon Sodom and upon Gomorrah brimstone and fire from the LORD out of heaven; -- Gen 19:24

Another case would be where Moses and a group of others saw God:

Then went up Moses, and Aaron, Nadab, and Abihu, and seventy of the elders of Israel: And

**they saw the God of Israel: and there was
under his feet as it were a paved work of a
sapphire stone, and as it were the body of
heaven in his clearness. -- Exo 24:9-10**

Jesus Christ as the angel of the Lord

As explicit as it is, the fact that the Lord Jesus
Christ is the angel of the Lord is not just established by
the above deduction. In spite of enough collaborating
evidence in the Bible to substantiate our thesis, some
"Christian" expositors still just can not get it:

Later Christian theology tended to see the preincarnate Christ in this figure (hence the definite article),
but the phrase probably referred vaguely to any
mediator sent by God.[10]

The evidence for the view that the angel of the Lord
is a preincarnate appearance of Christ is basically
analogical and falls short of being conclusive. The NT
does not clearly make that identification. It is best to
see the angel as a self-manifestation of Yahweh in a
form that would communicate his immanence and
direct concern to those to whom he ministered.[11]

There are some details about the angel of the Lord in the
Old Testament that further illuminate the identity of
the angel of the Lord.

The first occurs In the account of Jacob wrestling
with **"a man"** (Gen 32:24) who is identified as the angel
of the Lord (Hosea 12:4):

**And Jacob was left alone; and there wrestled a
man with him until the breaking of the day.
And when he saw that he prevailed not against
him, he touched the hollow of his thigh; and
the hollow of Jacob's thigh was out of joint, as
he wrestled with him. And he said, Let me go,
for the day breaketh. And he said, I will not let
thee go, except thou bless me. And he said unto
him, What is thy name? And he said, Jacob.
And he said, Thy name shall be called no more
Jacob, but Israel: for as a prince hast thou
power with God and with men, and hast
prevailed. And Jacob asked him, and said, Tell**

> me, I pray thee, thy name. And he said,
> Wherefore is it that thou dost ask after my
> name? And he blessed him there. And Jacob
> called the name of the place Peniel: for I have
> seen God face to face, and my life is preserved.
> -- Gen 32:24-30

It should be obvious that the angel of the Lord did not
ask Jacob his name because he did not know who he
was; he queried him because of the trouble that Jacob
had remembering his name on an earlier occasion:

> And he came unto his father, and said, My
> father: and he said, Here am I; who art thou,
> my son? And Jacob said unto his father, I am
> Esau thy firstborn; I have done according as
> thou badest me: arise, I pray thee, sit and eat of
> my venison, that thy soul may bless me. -- Gen
> 27:18-19

But it is the response of the angel of the Lord when
Jacob asked him his name that is worth noting:
**"Wherefore is it that thou dost ask after my
name?"** (Gen 32:29). Notice also that the angel of the
Lord **"blessed him"** (Gen 32:29) of whom the children
get their name. This is significant considering what
Peter later said to the children of Israel:

> Ye are the children of the prophets, and of the
> covenant which God made with our fathers,
> saying unto Abraham, And in thy seed shall all
> the kindreds of the earth be blessed. Unto you
> first God, having raised up his Son Jesus, sent
> him to bless you, in turning away every one of
> you from his iniquities. -- Acts 3:25-26

The next relevant account of the angel of the Lord is
a mention of him to Moses by God:

> Behold, I send an Angel before thee, to keep
> thee in the way, and to bring thee into the
> place which I have prepared. Beware of him,
> and obey his voice, provoke him not; for he will
> not pardon your transgressions: for my name is
> in him. But if thou shalt indeed obey his voice,
> and do all that I speak; then I will be an enemy

unto thine enemies, and an adversary unto thine adversaries. For mine Angel shall go before thee, and bring thee in unto the Amorites, and the Hittites, and the Perizzites, and the Canaanites, the Hivites, and the Jebusites: and I will cut them off. -- Exo 23:20-23

Attention should be paid once again to the emphasis on a name. Here the angel of the Lord is said to have God's **"name in him"** (Gen 23:21). The same is true of the Lord Jesus Christ:

Behold, a virgin shall be with child, and shall bring forth a son, and they shall call his name Emmanuel, which being interpreted is, God with us. -- Mat 1:23

Wherefore God also hath highly exalted him, and given him a name which is above every name: That at the name of Jesus every knee should bow, of things in heaven, and things in earth, and things under the earth; -- Phil 2:9-10

Not only was God's **"name in him"** (Gen 23:21), but the angel of the Lord was God's presence:

And he said, My presence shall go with thee, and I will give thee rest. -- Exo 33:14

We are thine: thou never barest rule over them; they were not called by thy name. -- Isa 63:19

The Lord Jesus Christ is also connected with the presence of God:

Repent ye therefore, and be converted, that your sins may be blotted out, when the times of refreshing shall come from the presence of the Lord; And he shall send Jesus Christ, which before was preached unto you: -- Acts 3:20

For Christ is not entered into the holy places made with hands, which are the figures of the true; but into heaven itself, now to appear in the presence of God for us: -- Heb 9:24

It is also pertinent to consider that the children of Israel were enjoined to **"beware of him, and obey his voice, provoke him not"** (Exo 23:21). The same could be said for sinners who reject the Lord Jesus Christ:

> **And to you who are troubled rest with us,
> when the Lord Jesus shall be revealed from
> heaven with his mighty angels, In flaming fire
> taking vengeance on them that know not God,
> and that obey not the gospel of our Lord Jesus
> Christ: -- 2 Th 1:7-8**

And finally, but not last in importance or assistance, the
angel of the Lord, it is here acknowledged, has the
authority to pardon transgressions. This was also true of
the Lord Jesus Christ:

> **When Jesus saw their faith, he said unto the
> sick of the palsy, Son, thy sins be forgiven thee.
> -- Mark 2:5**

> **And when he saw their faith, he said unto him,
> Man, thy sins are forgiven thee. -- Luke 5:20**

The next principal appearance of the angel of the
Lord was his manifestation to Joshua. The Lord had just
spoken to Joshua four times (Josh 1:1, 3:7, 4:1,15) before
he had this encounter:

> **And it came to pass, when Joshua was by
> Jericho, that he lifted up his eyes and looked,
> and, behold, there stood a man over against
> him with his sword drawn in his hand: and
> Joshua went unto him, and said unto him, Art
> thou for us, or for our adversaries? And he
> said, Nay; but as captain of the host of the
> LORD am I now come. And Joshua fell on his
> face to the earth, and did worship, and said
> unto him, What saith my lord unto his servant?
> And the captain of the LORD'S host said unto
> Joshua, Loose thy shoe from off thy foot; for
> the place whereon thou standest is holy. And
> Joshua did so. -- Josh 5:13-15**

Once again the accent is on the name of the angel of the
Lord. He is called **"the captain of the Lord's host"**
(Josh 5:15) while the Lord Jesus Christ is similarly
termed:

> **For it became him, for whom are all things, and**

> by whom are all things, in bringing many sons
> unto glory, to make the captain of their salva-
> tion perfect through sufferings. -- Heb 2:10

Observe also that this **"captain"** accepted worship, both
here and in the New Testament:

> And, behold, there came a leper and wor-
> shipped him, saying, Lord, if thou wilt, thou
> canst make me clean. And Jesus put forth his
> hand, and touched him, saying, I will; be thou
> clean. And immediately his leprosy was
> cleansed. -- Mat 8:2-3

> And as they went to tell his disciples, behold,
> Jesus met them, saying, All hail. And they came
> and held him by the feet, and worshipped him.
> -- Mat 28:9

Another instance in which question concerning the
name of the angel of the Lord unveils his identity is
found in his appearance to Manoah and his wife:

> And Manoah said unto the angel of the LORD, I
> pray thee, let us detain thee, until we shall
> have made ready a kid for thee. And the angel
> of the LORD said unto Manoah, Though thou
> detain me, I will not eat of thy bread: and if
> thou wilt offer a burnt offering, thou must offer
> it unto the LORD. For Manoah knew not that
> he was an angel of the LORD. And Manoah said
> unto the angel of the LORD, What is thy name,
> that when thy sayings come to pass we may do
> thee honour? And the angel of the LORD said
> unto him, Why askest thou thus after my name,
> seeing it is secret? So Manoah took a kid with a
> meat offering, and offered it upon a rock unto
> the LORD: and the angel did wonderously; and
> Manoah and his wife looked on. For it came to
> pass, when the flame went up toward heaven
> from off the altar, that the angel of the LORD
> ascended in the flame of the altar. And Manoah
> and his wife looked on it, and fell on their faces
> to the ground. -- Judg 13:15-20

Here the angel of the Lord specifically relates that he
will not give his name because it is **"secret"** (Judg

13:18). But notice also that the angel did **"wonderously"** (Judg 13:19). Although the works of God are said to
be wonderful (Psa 107:8; Isa 25:1), there is only one
person who can claim the title:

> **For unto us a child is born, unto us a son is
> given: and the government shall be upon his
> shoulder: and his name shall be called Wonder-
> ful, Counsellor, The mighty God, The everlast-
> ing Father, The Prince of Peace. -- Isa 9:6**

The New Testament likewise furnishes us with the
particulars that establish the identity of the angel of the
Lord. The first is an analogy given by Paul:

> **And my temptation which was in my flesh ye
> despised not, nor rejected; but received me as
> an angel of God, even as Christ Jesus. -- Gal
> 4:14**

The second is an actual event that took place:

> **For there stood by me this night the angel of
> God, whose I am, and whom I serve, Saying,
> Fear not, Paul; thou must be brought before
> Caesar: and, lo, God hath given thee all them
> that sail with thee. Wherefore, sirs, be of good
> cheer: for I believe God, that it shall be even as
> it was told me. -- Acts 27:25**

Paul did not say that he was a servant of the God
represented by the angel, he said that he was a servant
of the angel. And, as we have seen, this was none other
than the Lord Jesus Christ:

> **Paul, a servant of Jesus Christ, called to be an
> apostle, separated unto the gospel of God, --
> Rom 1:1**

This brings up the question of the angel of the Lord in
the New Testament.

The angel of the Lord in the New Testament

That the angel of the Lord in the Old Testament was
a preincarnate revelation of the Lord Jesus Christ is
without reservation, but what of the New Testament?

Specifically those references to the angel of the Lord during the personal advent of the Lord Jesus Christ. The designation *the angel of the Lord* occurs nine times in the New Testament while the similar title *an angel of the Lord* appears three times. Another relevant phrase, *angel of God,* is found twice as *an angel of God* and once as *the angel of God.* The specific passages in question are naturally found in the Gospels:

> **But while he thought on these things, behold, the angel of the Lord appeared unto him in a dream, saying, Joseph, thou son of David, fear not to take unto thee Mary thy wife: for that which is conceived in her is of the Holy Ghost. -- Mat 1:20**

> **Then Joseph being raised from sleep did as the angel of the Lord had bidden him, and took unto him his wife: -- Mat 1:24**

> **And when they were departed, behold, the angel of the Lord appeareth to Joseph in a dream, saying, Arise, and take the young child and his mother, and flee into Egypt, and be thou there until I bring thee word: for Herod will seek the young child to destroy him. -- Mat 2:13**

> **And, behold, there was a great earthquake: for the angel of the Lord descended from heaven, and came and rolled back the stone from the door, and sat upon it. -- Mat 28:2**

> **And, lo, the angel of the Lord came upon them, and the glory of the Lord shone round about them: and they were sore afraid. -- Luke 2:9**

The identity here of the angel of the Lord presents an apparent problem to some:

> Appearances of the Angel cease after the incarnation of Christ.[12]

> Not *"the"* angel, but *an* angel. The Authorized Version is incorrect in using several times in the New Testament the definite article.[13]

> Certainly the "angel of the Lord" in Luke 2:9 is not Christ.[14]

> The angel of the Lord spoken of in the NT must not
> be confounded with the OT Angel of Jahweh.[15]

There are four possible explanations for the identity
of the angel of the Lord in the New Testament: an
ordinary angel, the angel Gabriel, the Lord Jesus Christ,
or a combination of any of them. First, the opinion that
the angel of the Lord in the New Testament was just an
ordinary angel. The usage of the term *the angel of the
Lord* in the Old Testament is of no help, for as we have
seen in the previous chapters, the angel of the Lord in
the Old Testament was always the genuine angel of the
Lord. Likewise, the six references to *an angel of the Lord*
in the Old Testament were identified in the context as
the angel of the Lord. And once in the New Testament
(Acts 7:30), a mention of an angel of the Lord is also
distinguished as the angel of the Lord by comparison
with the original account in the Old Testament (Exo
3:2). Another reference to an angel of the Lord in the
New Testament (Luke 1:11) makes it clear that the
angel Gabriel is in view (Luke 1:19). The final report of
an angel of the Lord in the New Testament (Mat 2:19) is
undoubtedly the same as the angel who also appeared to
Joseph in a dream (Mat 1:20, 2:13). Therefore, if the
angel of the Lord in the New Testament is just an
ordinary angel, it is a usage restricted to the New
Testament. However, **"an angel of God"** (Acts 10:3)
that came to Cornelius certainly appears to be just an
common angel.

As just mentioned, the angel Gabriel was referred to
as an angel of the Lord (Luke 1:11). It is he who is
connected with Christ's birth in that he appeared to
Zacharias, and named John the Baptist, the forerunner
of the Lord Jesus Christ (Luke 1:13), and to Mary,
telling her the name *Jesus* for her son (Luke 1:31). There
are four similarities between the angel of the Lord in
Matthew and the mission of the angel Gabriel. The first
two involve the mention and naming of a son:

And she shall bring forth a son, and thou shalt

> **call his name JESUS: for he shall save his people from their sins. -- Mat 1:21**

> **And, behold, thou shalt conceive in thy womb, and bring forth a son, and shalt call his name JESUS. -- Luke 1:31**

Both angels also mention the supernatural nature of Mary's conception:

> **But while he thought on these things, behold, the angel of the Lord appeared unto him in a dream, saying, Joseph, thou son of David, fear not to take unto thee Mary thy wife: for that which is conceived in her is of the Holy Ghost. -- Mat 1:20**

> **And the angel answered and said unto her, The Holy Ghost shall come upon thee, and the power of the Highest shall overshadow thee: therefore also that holy thing which shall be born of thee shall be called the Son of God. -- Luke 1:35**

And both angels connect this supernatural son with God:

> **Behold, a virgin shall be with child, and shall bring forth a son, and they shall call his name Emmanuel, which being interpreted is, God with us. -- Mat 1:23**

> **And the angel answered and said unto her, The Holy Ghost shall come upon thee, and the power of the Highest shall overshadow thee: therefore also that holy thing which shall be born of thee shall be called the Son of God. -- Luke 1:35**

For this same reason it is also plausible that Gabriel is the angel of the Lord who appeared to the **"shepherds abiding in the field"** (Luke 2:9) at the birth of **"Christ the Lord"** (Luke 2:11). Although the angel of the Lord mentioned in these accounts could be Gabriel, there is no such evidence that the other mentions of the angel of the Lord could be him as well (Mat 28:2; Acts 5:19, 8:26, 12:7, 12:23). There would also be no reason to assume that **"an angel of God"** (Acts 10:3) who came to

Cornelius was likewise the angel Gabriel.

We have left to consider whether or not the angel of the Lord in the New Testament could be the Lord Jesus Christ or a combination of one of our options. It has already been pointed out that both **"the angel of God"** (Acts 27:23) and **"an angel of God"** (Gal 4:14) are in fact the Lord Jesus Christ. There are then two classes of verses to consider: those that refer to the angel of the Lord during the advent of Christ and those after his advent. Of the first the question is inevitably asked: how could Jesus Christ as the angel of the Lord appear to Joseph in a dream (Mat 1:20, 2:13), speak to the shepherds (Luke 2:9), and roll back the stone from Christ's tomb (Mat 28:2) if he was already on the earth at that time? The only way he could is revealed in his discourse to Nicodemus:

> **And no man hath ascended up to heaven, but he that came down from heaven, even the Son of man which is in heaven. -- John 3:13**

The other references in the New Testament to the angel of the Lord are naturally more apt to be considered as relating to the Lord Jesus Christ since he had already ascended back to heaven:

> **But the angel of the Lord by night opened the prison doors, and brought them forth, and said, -- Acts 5:19**

> **And the angel of the Lord spake unto Philip, saying, Arise, and go toward the south unto the way that goeth down from Jerusalem unto Gaza, which is desert. -- Acts 8:26**

> **And, behold, the angel of the Lord came upon him, and a light shined in the prison: and he smote Peter on the side, and raised him up, saying, Arise up quickly. And his chains fell off from his hands. -- Acts 12:7**

> **And immediately the angel of the Lord smote him, because he gave not God the glory: and he was eaten of worms, and gave up the ghost. -- Acts 12:23**

If there is any problem with these referring to the Lord Jesus Christ it should be remembered that he later appears as a **"mighty angel"** (Rev 10:1) who takes credit for the two witnesses who prophesy during the Tribulation. So who is the angel of the Lord in the New Testament? It is entirely possible that an ordinary angel, the angel Gabriel, and the Lord Jesus Christ are all spoken of as the angel of the Lord with each appearing in one or more passages.

Jesus Christ as God

Regardless of the identity of the angel of the Lord in those few passages where he is mentioned in the New Testament, the deity of the angel of the Lord provides us with absolute proof for the deity of the Lord Jesus Christ. But this is only the beginning, for the Bible abounds with so much evidence for his deity that you would have to deliberately miss it to not see it. Since the deity of the Lord Jesus Christ can be demonstrated and verified in so many different ways as to be almost ineffable, we submit only the main proofs so as to supplement the indisputable and undeniable testimony of his deity as seen in the accounts of the angel of the Lord.

This concise analysis of the deity of the Lord Jesus Christ can be classified as to confirmation for his deity as seen in his works and affirmation of his deity as related to his person. Of his divine works, his identification as the creator stands at the forefront:

> **All things were made by him; and without him was not any thing made that was made. -- John 1:3**

> **For by him were all things created, that are in heaven, and that are in earth, visible and invisible, whether they be thrones, or dominions, or principalities, or powers: all things were created by him, and for him: -- Col 1:16**

Closely aligned with this is his providence:

> **And he is before all things, and by him all things consist. -- Col 1:17**

> **Who being the brightness of his glory, and the express image of his person, and upholding all things by the word of his power, when he had by himself purged our sins, sat down on the right hand of the Majesty on high; -- Heb 1:3**

Two of his works in relation to man further reveal his deity:

> **And, behold, they brought to him a man sick of the palsy, lying on a bed: and Jesus seeing their faith said unto the sick of the palsy; Son, be of good cheer; thy sins be forgiven thee. -- Mat 9:2**

> **For the Father judgeth no man, but hath committed all judgment unto the Son: -- John 5:22**

His command over the physical realm likewise manifests his supernatural credentials:

> **And he saith unto them, Why are ye fearful, O ye of little faith? Then he arose, and rebuked the winds and the sea; and there was a great calm. -- Mat 8:26**

> **When the ruler of the feast had tasted the water that was made wine, and knew not whence it was: (but the servants which drew the water knew;) the governor of the feast called the bridegroom, -- John 2:9**

The works done by the Lord Jesus Christ wrought admiration and certified that he was sent from God:

> **And when the sabbath day was come, he began to teach in the synagogue: and many hearing him were astonished, saying, From whence hath this man these things? and what wisdom is this which is given unto him, that even such mighty works are wrought by his hands? -- Mark 6:2**

> **But I have greater witness than that of John: for the works which the Father hath given me to finish, the same works that I do, bear**

**witness of me, that the Father hath sent me. --
John 5:36**

He was therefore the object of worship reserved for God
alone:

> **Then they that were in the ship came and
> worshipped him, saying, Of a truth thou art the
> Son of God. -- Mat 14:33**

> **And again, when he bringeth in the firstbegot-
> ten into the world, he saith, And let all the
> angels of God worship him. -- Heb 1:6**

The person of the Lord Jesus Christ was declared to
be divine and identified with God himself. This is
accomplished throughout the Bible in a variety of ways.
One of which is the employment of the same titles as
God. They are both said to be the Saviour:

> **Yet I am the LORD thy God from the land of
> Egypt, and thou shalt know no god but me: for
> there is no saviour beside me. -- Hosea 13:4**

> **For our conversation is in heaven; from
> whence also we look for the Saviour, the Lord
> Jesus Christ: -- Phil 3:20**

They are each called the Rock:

> **He is the Rock, his work is perfect: for all his
> ways are judgment: a God of truth and without
> iniquity, just and right is he. -- Deu 32:4**

> **And did all drink the same spiritual drink: for
> they drank of that spiritual Rock that followed
> them: and that Rock was Christ. -- 1 Cor 10:4**

They are both termed the Holy One:

> **To whom then will ye liken me, or shall I be
> equal? saith the Holy One. -- Isa 40:25**

> **Because thou wilt not leave my soul in hell,
> neither wilt thou suffer thine Holy One to see
> corruption. -- Acts 2:27**

And finally, they are each declared to be the Redeemer:

> **Thus saith the LORD, thy Redeemer, the Holy
> One of Israel; I am the LORD thy God which**

teacheth thee to profit, which leadeth thee by the way that thou shouldest go. -- Isa 48:17

Forasmuch as ye know that ye were not redeemed with corruptible things, as silver and gold, from your vain conversation received by tradition from your fathers; But with the precious blood of Christ, as of a lamb without blemish and without spot: -- 1 Pet 1:18-19

Another way in which the deity of the Lord Jesus Christ is substantiated is by those references to him in the New Testament that distinctly refer to God in the Old Testament. Both God and the Son of God claimed to be the I AM (Exo 3:14; John 8:58), the judge of the heathen (Joel 3:12; Mat 25:32), the Lord of lord's (Psa 136:3; Rev 19:16), and the first and the last (Isa 44:6; Rev 22:13). John the Baptist prepared the way of the Lord (Isa 40:3), who is identified as the Lord Jesus Christ (Mat 3:3). Every knee will bow to God (Isa 45:23) in the person of the Lord Jesus Christ (Phil 2:10-11).

The most conclusive and irrefutable proof, however, for the deity of the Lord Jesus Christ is when he is directly called God:

In the beginning was the Word, and the Word was with God, and the Word was God. -- John 1:1

Whose are the fathers, and of whom as concerning the flesh Christ came, who is over all, God blessed for ever. Amen. -- Rom 9:5

And we know that the Son of God is come, and hath given us an understanding, that we may know him that is true, and we are in him that is true, even in his Son Jesus Christ. This is the true God, and eternal life. -- 1 John 5:20

So although a study of the angel of the Lord provides us with one of the greatest proofs that **"God was manifest in the flesh"** (1 Tim 3:16), such testimony is consistent with that found throughout the whole Bible.

FOOTNOTES

CHAPTER TWO

1. Mortimer J. Adler, *The Angels and Us* (New York: Macmillan Publishing Co., 1982), p.44.
2. Ibid.
3. *New Catholic Encyclopedia* (New York: McGraw-Hill Book Company, 1967), p.511.
4. Ibid.
5. Ibid.
6. Ibid.
7. *The Encyclopedia of Judaism* (New York: Macmillan Publishing Co., 1989), p.59.
8. *The New Encyclopedia Britannica,* 15th edition (Chicago: Encyclopedia Britannica), p.399.
9. Gustav Davidson, *A Dictionary of Angels* (New York: The Free Press, 1967), p.24.
10. Ibid., p.xix.
11. Encyclopedia of Judaism, p.58.
12. Davidson, p.184.
13. Adler, p.19,101.
14. Davidson, p.xviii.
15. Charles C. Ryrie, *Basic Theology* (Wheaton: Victor Books, 1986), p.129.
16. Ibid.
17. Theodora V.W. Ward, *Men and Angels* (New York: The Viking Press, 1969), p.52.
18. Ryrie, p.129.
19. Encyclopedia Britannica, p.400.

20. Ibid.

21. Ward, p.31.

22. Arno Clemens Gaebelein, *The Angels of God* (New York: Our Hope, 1924), p.20.

23. Adler, p.44.

24. Ibid., p.43.

25. Ibid., p.46.

26. Ibid.

27. Ibid.

28. Davidson, p.xxiii.

29. C. Fred Dickason, *Angels, Elect and Evil* (Chicago: Moody Press, 1975), p.38,61; Louis Berkhof, *Systematic Theology* (Grand Rapids: Wm. B. Eerdmans Publishing Co., 1941), p.146; Herry C. Thiessen, *Introductory Lectures in Systematic Theology* (Grand Rapids: Wm. B. Eerdmans Publishing Co., 1949), p.197; Paul P. Enns, *The Moody Handbook of Theology* (Chicago: Moody Press, 1989); Adler, p.44; Encyclopedia of Judaism, p.58.

30. Adler, p.44.

31. Berkhof, p.146; Enns, p.290; Thiessen, p.198; Dickason, p.31,35,65; Adler, p.44; Encyclopedia of Judaism, p.58.

32. Adler, p.45.

33. Billy Graham, *Angels: God's Secret Agents,* rev. and expand. ed, (Waco: Word Books, 1986), p.9; Gaebelein, p.35; Dickason, p.30,150; Enns, p.294.

34. Dickason, p.30,118.

35. Ibid., p.60.

36. Ibid., p.117.

37. Ibid., p.59.

38. Ibid., p.58.

39. Ibid., p.35,59.

40. Enns, p.287; Dickason, p.60.

41. Dickason, p.25,36.

42. Ibid., p.61.

43. Dickason, p.87; Berkhof, p.146.

44. Dickason, p.87; Berkhof, p.146.

45. Dickason, p.87.

46. Ibid.

47. Adler, p.84; Graham, p.42; Ryrie, p.158; Dickason, p.33,76,158; Thiessen, p.208; Enns, p.296.

48. Adler, p.44.

49. Ibid., p.45.

50. Graham, p.41; Davidson, p.xx.

51. Davidson, p.352.

52. Dickason, p.32.

53. Gaebelein, p.16; Dickason, p.34; Davidson, p.xxi.

54. Dickason, p.34.

55. Ibid.

56. Ryrie, p.126; Dickason, p.35.

57. Adler, p.71.

58. Ryrie, p.126; Dickason, p.36.

59. Adler, p.12,27,36.

60. Adler, p.12.

61. Catholic Encyclopedia, p.509.

62. Ward, p.62.

CHAPTER FOUR

1. Elwell, p.47.

2. Ibid.

3. Ibid., p.48-49.

4. Madeleine S. Miller and J. Lane Miller, eds. *Harper's Bible Dictionary,* 8th ed. (New York: Harper & Row, 1973), p.19.

5. Davidson, p.24.

6. Encyclopedia of Judaism, p.58.

7. Alan F. Johnson and Robert E. Webber, *What Christians Believe* (Grand Rapids: Zondervan Publishing House, 1993), p.107.

8. *The Interpreter's Dictionary of the Bible* (Nashville: Abingdon Press, 1962), p.51.

9. James Hastings, ed. *Dictionary of the Bible* (New York: Charles Scribners' Sons, 1948), p.33-34.

10. Bruce M. Metzger and Michael D. Coogan, eds. *The Oxford Companion to the Bible* (New York: Oxford University Press, 1993), p.28.

11. Elwell, p.48.

12. Ryrie, p.130.

13. Gaebelein, p.65.

14. Elwell, p.47.

15. Hastings, p.33.

BIBLIOGRAPHY

Adler, Mortimer J. *The Angels and Us.* New York: Macmillan Publishing Co., 1982.

Berkhof, Louis. *Systematic Theology.* Grand Rapids: Wm. B. Eerdmans Publishing Co., 1941.

Davidson, Gustav. *A Dictionary of Angels.* New York: The Free Press, 1967.

Dickason, C. Fred. *Angels, Elect and Evil.* Chicago: Moody Press, 1975.

Elwell, Walter A., ed. *Evangelical Dictionary of Theology.* Grand Rapids: Baker Book House, 1984.

Enns, Paul P. *The Moody Handbook of Theology.* Chicago: Moody Press, 1989.

Gaebelein, Arno Clemens. *The Angels of God.* New York: Our Hope, 1924.

Gill, John. *A Complete Body of Doctrinal and Practical Divinity.* London: Mathews & Leigh, 1809; reprint, Paris: The Baptist Standard Banner, 1987.

Graham, Billy. *Angels: God's Secret Agents,* rev. and exp. ed. Waco: Word Books, 1986.

Hastings, James, ed. *Dictionary of the Bible.* New York: Charles Scribners' Sons, 1948.

Johnson, Alan F., and Webber, Robert E. *What Christians Believe.* Grand Rapids: Zondervan Publishing House, 1993.

Metzger, Bruce M. and Coogan, Michael D., eds. *The Oxford Companion to the Bible.* New York: Oxford University Press, 1993.

Miller, Madeleine S. and Miller, J. Lane, eds. *Harper's Bible Dictionary,* 8th ed. New York: Harper & Row, 1973.

New Catholic Encyclopedia. New York: McGraw-Hill Book Company, 1967.

Ryrie, Charles C. *Basic Theology.* Wheaton: Victor Books, 1986.

The Encyclopedia of Judaism. New York: Macmillan Publishing Co., 1989.

The Interpreter's Dictionary of the Bible. Nashville: Abingdon Press, 1962.

The New Encyclopedia Britannica, 15th edition. Chicago: Encyclopedia Britannica, 1991.

Thiessen, Henry C. *Introductory Lectures in Systematic Theology.* Grand Rapids: Wm. B. Eerdmans Publishing Co., 1949.

Ward, Theodora V. W. *Men and Angels.* New York: The Viking Press, 1969.

INDEX OF SCRIPTURES